Table of Contents

Introduction

As a child, I was very angry. My parents used to marvel at my anger because it was so consuming and overwhelming for a child. Everyone avoided playing or even fighting with me; friends, family, and other people.

My parents thought at first that this was normal child behavior, which I would outgrow as an adult. However, I got even worse once I became a teenager. I remember breaking my favorite toy once because my brother chastised me for doing something I considered trivial.

As much as I was expressive about my anger, it wasn't something I really enjoyed. It made me really uncomfortable, but I couldn't stop being angry, no matter how much I secretly tried.

I have to admit that anger made me feel powerful, especially because people learned to leave me alone. No one touched my things for fear of being yelled at. It was amusing and satisfying.

But, as I grew older, I understood how lonely and empty anger had made me. I had no friends and the few I had, I couldn't really call friends. I couldn't work in one place for long without being fired.

One day, I came to the realization that I had to do something about my anger. So, I decided to go for therapy after reading a lot of books and materials on anger management.

That single decision changed my life and improved it for the best because I am now a much better person than I was. My life is better than it used to be. I now have friends who wouldn't trade our relationship for anything, and my relationship with my parents is way better than it used to be. I am happy.

If you can relate to my story, it means you have a problem with anger management as I used to, and you are reading this right now because you want a better life for yourself.

In itself, anger is not a problem. But, the inability to manage anger is a major problem many of us contend with. Like thousands of other people, you have probably tried everything to gain control of your emotions without success.

Well, I want to congratulate you if you are reading this book right now. This is a life-changing book that I have written on effective anger management using all the knowledge I gained from therapy and extensive research with my own personal experiences.

This book is laden with practical and workable solutions that other books probably don't offer. Consider this book your one-stop-shop to everything you need to know about anger and anger management.

I start the book by talking extensively on the emotion itself. What is anger? Is it negative or positive? What are the things everyone should know about anger? These are some of the important questions I answered in the first chapter of the book.

I also talked about the cause of anger and the factors that fuel the experience of anger and its physiological responses. I also explained some of the most common myths about anger and why you shouldn't believe them.

In this book, I touched all the important aspects of anger management like the impact of culture and gender on anger expression, the different anger management exercises and techniques, CBT, and Emotional intelligence.

The most important part of this book is the 10 step guide to immediate and effective anger management, which you will find in no other book.

Of course, I can go on and on about what you should expect in "Anger management," but I will only be delaying you from seeing the goodness awaiting you in the book for yourself.

This book promises to be like no other you have read. So, why don't you grab a seat and let's get you started on the journey to a life devoid of anger, stress, anxiety, unhappiness, and turbulence?

Pick a copy for yourself and start reading your way to emotional intelligence and control!

Chapter One

The Basics of Anger

I like to think of anger as a subjective emotion, even though it is something we all experience as humans. Anger may be a universal emotion, but it is also subjective and unique to each individual. What makes you angry may not make another person angry. This is one thing about anger, which many people fail to understand.

How humans experience anger differs greatly, with varying degrees of intensity, duration, and frequency. The anger threshold of each person also varies, including how comfortable they are with feelings of anger. Some people are in a constant state of anger, while others rarely get angry unless they are deeply provoked.

Anger as an emotion may range from mild annoyance to extreme wrath or rage. According to the dictionary, anger is "a strong feeling of displeasure or hostility." From this definition, you can already tell that anger is something that you experience when something doesn't happen the way you would like.

Although you may consider anger an unwanted emotion, it is actually very natural. I have met so many people who think anger is an abominable emotion, which they must never be caught expressing or experiencing. This is understandable, considering the way the society and the world at large view anger.

However, anger experts largely describe this emotion as a basic and natural emotion that exists to promote and ensure human survival, evolving through years of human development. Anger is an emotion meant to protect you from perceived danger, harm, or hurt.

There are so many basic things people fail to understand about anger, and this inability to understand anger fuels the misconception many have about anger. To fully learn anger management, it is important first to understand anger as an emotion. This is a basic requirement for anger management because, like I always say, there is no way you can control something you don't understand.

Firstly, you need to understand that anger is a basic emotion. According to psychologists, basic emotions are those emotions that are universally associated and recognized with certain facial expressions.

Apart from anger, the other basic emotions are fear, joy, sadness, contempt, and surprise. One thing common to all of these emotions is that they have specific facial expressions that are recognized with them. When a person is angry, you can usually tell from their facial expression.

Another thing about anger and other basic emotions is that they usually come with specific behavioral responses. However, they may also trigger other expressions besides the universally recognized facial expressions, physiological responses, and behavioral responses.

Anger is also a largely misunderstood emotion, which is often confused with aggression. While you may think that anger is an unhealthy emotion, it is, in fact, healthy and very different from aggression or violence. Anger becomes aggressive or violent, depending on how you react to it.

I will talk more about this as we progress in the book, but one difference to keep in mind about anger and aggression is that aggression usually comes with an intent to harm someone or something while anger is an emotion that you experience when you are wrongly treated.

Contrary to what you may think, like many other people, anger is not an inherently bad or negative emotion. The belief that anger is a bad emotion is a general misconception most people have about anger. However, anger is a normal emotion; it is valuable and crucial to human survival.

You can also express anger in different ways, depending on your choice and reaction to anger. One of the many reasons why most people confuse aggression and anger is because they believe anger can only be expressed aggressively or violently. However, you can express anger in a variety of healthy and nonaggressive ways.

Anger FAQ (Frequently Asked Questions)

In the quest to understand anger, there are certain commonly asked questions that people pose to anger experts. Knowing the answers to these questions gives you a more open insight towards both anger and anger management. I'll be talking about these questions and providing suitable answers in order to help further you understand this emotion and the big misconception about it.

• *Why do I get angry?*

This is one of the most common questions asked about anger. Yes, why do you get angry? Naturally, you experience anger when you perceive a wrong or unjust situation. People get angry when they feel they have been treated unjustly, or a situation is unfair to them.

In fact, being in an unpleasant situation even further aggravates anger because the more you think about the whole unjustness of the situation, the angrier it makes you.

• *When do I get angry?*

Several factors affect which situation triggers an individual's anger, but one thing, which mostly determines when you get angry, is your interpretation of an anger-inducing situation. The interpretation you give to a situation also determines the intensity and duration of your anger.

• *Is anger problematic?*

Anger may be problematic or not, depending on your interpretation of a situation and the reaction it elicits. Not all anger is problematic.

There are types of anger that are genuinely aimed at solving a problem or righting a wrong.

Anger, in fact, serves a motivating force for confronting injustice. Anger is unproblematic because it is a natural emotion meant to alert you to danger and motivate you to respond. The only thing that determines whether anger becomes problematic or not is the response you give to the emotion.

- *Is anger bad?*

I will talk more about the perceived 'badness' of anger, but in itself, anger is not a bad emotion. You can even say that there is nothing such as a bad or good emotion. Emotions are natural bodily responses; they can't be bad or good in themselves.

When you experience anger, it is because you are meant to experience it, not because you are a bad person, or the anger is a bad feeling.

- *How can I know if I have an anger problem?*

As a universally-experienced emotion, everyone feels angry from time to time. People usually experience anger without severe or damaging consequences. The best way for you to judge if you have an anger problem is to evaluate the severity of the consequences of your anger.

For example, if you always end up breaking a property or physically assaulting someone when you are angry, then it means you have an anger problem to manage.

Apart from the questions above, there are other commonly asked questions about anger, and as you continue to read, you will find your answers to all of the questions you have about anger and anger management.

Understanding Anger
As an Emotional and Physiological Response

Like all primary emotions, anger is experienced in the body and the mind. When anger is experienced in mind, it is an emotional state. When it is experienced in the body, it is a physiological state.

Anger is always experienced both as an emotional and physiological state. But, in its mild form, anger is usually more of an emotional response than a physiological response. When you experience mild irritation from someone accidentally spilling water on you, it may not trigger the series of physiological events associated with anger because it is in mind.

The series of physiological and bodily responses that occur when you are angry usually happens when the anger is more intense than normal.

Emotions begin in the part of the brain known as the Amygdala. The amygdala has the responsibility of identifying possible threats to which it alerts you so you can take immediate actions to protect yourself from the perceived threat or danger.

Your amygdala is so efficient at its job that it instantly spurs you to react even before your cortex i.e., the part of your brain responsible for thinking and judgment is able to evaluate the situation and initiate a reasonable reaction. The thing is, when your amygdala activates the "fight or flight" response, it overrides all other reactions or responses in your body.

In other words, your brain is programmed in a way that pushes you to react to a situation before you even consider the appropriateness of your action. This is why experts often suggest that the key to anger management is to learn to control impulses.

As an emotional response, anger is often unidentifiable. However, in the physiological state, anger is often very noticeable, with little or no control over the responses. Even when you are pretty good at controlling your display of anger, it is almost impossible (if not completely impossible) for you to control the physiological responses that occur when you are angry.

For many years, experts have studied the physiology of anger in order to understand the anger fully. Overall, they came to the conclusion that the person to be most affected by anger is always the person experiencing that anger.

This means when you get angry, and out of control, you are causing more harm to yourself than the object of your anger.

Moving on, as you start to experience anger, you feel your body's muscles start to tense up. During this period, there is something going on in your brain. Some neurotransmitter chemicals known as catecholamine is being released in your body, resulting in a burst of energy, which may last for several minutes before it subsides.

That burst of energy you experience at that moment is what fuels the common angry impulse that pushes you to take immediate actions geared at protecting yourself. At this same time, you feel your heart rate increase, your blood pressure accelerates, and your breathing quickens in pace.

You may also feel your face flush as the increased blood flow moves into your limbs, preparing you for possible physical action. Your attention becomes completely focused on the target of your anger, and you are unable to pay mind to anything else.

With immediate effect in that same moment, the brain releases more neurotransmitters and hormones (adrenaline, noradrenaline, etc.). This triggers a heightened state of arousal, which means your body is now prepared to fight.

The release of the adrenaline and noradrenaline, coupled with the fact that you acted before you allowed your cortex to think, is what makes your anger rage out of control. But, with your prefrontal cortex, you can learn to keep your emotions under control.

Just as the amygdala is in charge of emotions, the prefrontal cortex is also in charge of judgment. The left prefrontal cortex helps to rationalize emotional reactions by switching off your emotions when they become too intense.

Therefore, to gain control over your anger, you have to learn how to give your prefrontal cortex superiority over the amygdala so that you can stop reacting before you think carefully about a situation.

Just as there is a physiological reaction phase for your anger, you also experience a wind-down phase when the situation subsides, or the target of your anger is no longer in your environment. However, it is usually difficult for the physiological state of anger to subside even after the target is no longer on sight.

The state of arousal induced by the release of adrenaline when you are angry lasts for hours and sometimes daily, depending on the intensity of the situation, which triggered the anger. Unsurprisingly, this reduces your anger threshold, making it easier for you to get angry subsequently.

During the period in which you have your wind-down phase, you are more likely to get angry in response to trivial irritation and mild issues that usually wouldn't bother you that much. This continued state of arousal also leaves you in a state that makes it impossible to clearly remember the details of the event that made you angry.

Based on research, arousal has been confirmed to be very crucial to memory and recall; you need it for efficient remembering. But, arousal enhances memory and performance only when it is at a moderate level.

When arousal exceeds the optimum level required for concentration, memory, and performance, it renders your brain unable to form new memories. Anger is one of the emotions that normally induces high levels of arousal, which could go beyond the appropriate level. This affects your concentration and reduces your ability to remember details of your angry explosions correctly.

The Cycle of Stress, Anxiety, and Anger

There is a relationship between stress, anxiety, and anger, which you may not be aware of. Sometimes, the cause of a person's anger is actually nothing but stress or anxiety. If you are familiar with positive psychology, you may have learned that stress often leads to anxiety and vice versa.

Stress and anxiety also lead to anger, in many cases. Interestingly, anger has also been linked to anxiety and stress in some people. This points to why I call this chapter "The cycle." There is probably nothing better to describe the relationship between all three.

Anxiety and stress play a major role in anger, and they are also two of the most common anger triggers. An individual who is in a perpetually stressful or anxious state if more prone to anger than people who aren't.

One of the many reasons why there is a lot of negativity flying around in the world nowadays is because there are many stressors now than we had in the past. Technology and social media, as innovative as they are, are major stressors for many unsuspecting people.

Anger, anxiety, and stress are all emotional states that are triggered when the brain suspects a possibly harmful situation and activates the "fight or flight" response, so this may be the reason why all three are so closely related.

We all experience stress and anxiety because they are natural human emotions. However, there is one difference between stress and anxiety. Stress is the body's response to a perceived threat in the environment. For example, you may become stressed because you are working hard, and you aren't getting enough sleep.

In a situation like this, your body triggered stress because there is a perceived threat to the body, due to you not sleeping as you should. On the other hand, anxiety is regarded as a response to stress. So, anxiety is triggered when the stress response is on activation.

Let's say you have an examination coming up, and you have been working really hard, staying up late just to read. In other words, you are sacrificing your sleep to pass your examination. Naturally, fatigue will set in since you aren't sleeping enough, and your body is in a stressed state.

How would anxiety come in? You may become worried about your examination and start having doubts about your ability to pass the examination due to the stress you are feeling. You may not know it, but the stressed state you are in is what is inviting doubts about the possibility of you passing the examination.

In a state like this, it is quite easy to trigger anger since we already said that both stress and anxiety lead to anger. When you are stressed and feeling anxious about your coming examination, you may start getting irritated, annoyed, or fully angry at every slight irritation that comes your way. You may shout at your sibling for coming into your room while you are reading.

In the example above, you have allowed your feelings of stress and anxiety to transcend into a state of anger.

Something most people also don't know is that there are times when you aren't actually angry, but you are acting angry. This is when anger becomes a secondary emotion, as experts say. Sometimes, it isn't anger that you are actually feeling, but you are masking the real emotion, which could be anxiety with anger.

Anxiety is often associated with fear, worry, or doubt. But, experts have said that it is also common for anxiety to be accompanied by feelings of anger, usually subtle and underlying. Generally, anger is not regarded as a symptom of anxiety.

This is due to the fact that they are considered to be two different emotional responses. But, experts believe that both emotions can overlap since they have common cognitive and biological features.

The reason why you may fail to identify anxiety as the underlying emotion behind your anger is that anger is an instantaneous emotional response, something you feel immediately when there is a trigger.

Anxiety evolves into anger when a person is unable to address the cause of the anxiety directly. You may be covering your anxiety up with anger because you find the cause too painful to address directly. So, you project the emotion as anger instead.

There are many situations where anxiety can morph into anger, especially when it is in relation to an anxiety disorder. For example, an individual with Obsessive-Compulsive Disorder (OCD) may get angry when their ritualistic routine is interrupted by someone else. Anxiety is recognized as the primary emotion behind OCD as a disorder.

Fear has been identified to be the hidden emotion behind the anger in so many people, and as I already highlighted, anxiety is an emotion associated with fear and worry.

Many times, anger management is taken together with stress/anxiety management because there is no way an individual can learn to control anger without curtailing the plenty of stressors in their life first.

Anxiety, stress, and anger share a relationship that you will come to understand better as I talk about the factors that impact anger and the truth behind anger as a secondary emotion.

Factors That Cause and Trigger Anger

Because of its spontaneity, it's usually difficult to identify the trigger or cause of anger. It may even seem to you like your anger is coming out of nowhere. This is due to the level of intensity with which anger always surfaces; this eradicated the cause or trigger and left you perplexed.

Typically, you are often left with the consequence of your anger or the damage that has been done without any knowledge of what led to the anger in the first place. This kind of problem becomes a recurring pattern, especially with people who have an anger management problem.

I have seen instances where a person has an episode of explosive anger, and the next instant, they can't even remember why they exploded in the first place. Sometimes, they recognize the cause only after the explosion already happened, and then they feel remorseful because of the result.

It is quite easy for this to become a cycle or pattern. Most times, something happens, you get angry, you react explosively, calm down after a while, regret your angry reaction to the situation, and then repeat it all over in another situation. What makes it worse is that you make no effort to learn the cause of your anger, so you just remain in that disturbing pattern.

To learn anger management successfully, it is absolutely important to know the factors that could possibly be causing your anger. It is impossible to manage something if you don't even know the source of that thing.

You can't learn to control your anger if you don't identify and address the cause of the anger. For instance, if your anger is being induced by stress, but you fail to address the stressors in your life, it will be pretty difficult for you to control the anger even if you do go for anger management. As long as the stressors exist, you will continue to find yourself getting angry for the most ludicrous reasons.

Typically, anger is caused by people, situations, and circumstances that you find yourself, whether intentionally or not. Of these three, the most frequent cause of anger is people (especially those you share personal relationships with). Your partners, children, friends, and family members are some of those people that may constantly annoy you or make you angry.

This is understandable because your family, friends, and children are usually the ones you have your closest relationships with.

Moving on, there are several factors that could be the trigger or cause of your anger apart from people or situations. If you are someone who constantly gets angry no matter how trivial the situation is, it may not be because someone is always doing something to annoy you or the situation is usually provoking.

In many cases, the reason behind your anger may be something completely different from what you think. These reasons are usually something that you may not even think capable of riling you up.

For instance, if you get home from work on a tiring day and you feel something hit you just as you enter the house. On entering the room, you find that it is your 10-year old kid who threw the thing that hit you. If you shout at the child because you were hit, would you say that it is really because your child threw something at you?

Of course, it may seem like the cause of your anger is that you were hit by something your child threw. After all, how would you have gotten angry and shouted at the child if that didn't happen? However, the actual reason for your anger is the fact that you had a tiring day at work.

The stress you feel from work is what you needed an outlet to let out, and you chose to make that an opportunity to let out the stress. If you were coming home, free-spirited, energetic, and happy, you obviously wouldn't mind that something was thrown at you. In fact, you may even scoop the child in your arms and play around a little before proceeding inside.

So, there are sometimes certain factors triggering your anger underneath without your knowledge. Below, I'll be identifying and talking about some of the factors that could be causing or triggering your anger.

• Childhood and Upbringing

How a person reacts to anger or copes with feelings of anger is largely influenced by the kind of childhood and upbringing they had. There are cases where the reason behind a person's anger while growing up is that they learned it while growing up.

Growing up, many people learn about anger in a way that makes it difficult and sometimes impossible to manage as an adult. As a child, you may have grown up in an environment where anger is usually acted out violently or aggressively. So, you grow up with the mindset that this is the right way to show your anger.

With a mindset like this, you may find yourself unable to understand and manage your anger. So, you get angry at the slightest things. You may become angry because someone did something you don't like, even though you could have just approached them and talked about whatever they did. You may also have an episode of angry outbursts when you find yourself in a situation you don't like.

Another way your childhood or upbringing may be influencing your response to anger is if you grew up with the belief that repressing anger is the right way to 'express' it. Many people were raised to believe they are never to complain when they feel wronged or unjustly treated. They were also punished whenever they expressed anger as children.

If you were brought up like this, the result is that you end up learning to suppress your anger, which later becomes a major problem in adulthood, making you react to uncomfortable situations inappropriately. You may also turn your anger inward on yourself if you feel you shouldn't release your anger outside.

As a child, you may have grown up watching your parents and other relevant adults in your life act out of control when they are angry.

This may have taught you to see anger as something that is quite frightening and destructive.

Either of two things may happen; you may become terrified of anger as an emotion and become afraid of expressing your anger. This means even when something truly provocative happens, you bottle the anger in without expressing how you feel.

On the other hand, you may learn this behavior and also start acting like the adults you watched growing up. In the eventuality that you become afraid of getting angry, it is possible that the feelings of anger may resurface in situations that are completely unrelated.

For example, if you grow up in a family where your parents are always fighting and making up, you may grow up thinking of this as normal behavior and start exhibiting similar behaviors in your relationships, whether consciously or subconsciously. You may feel uncomfortable if you and your partner do not fight in the space of a week with the belief that something is wrong.

● *Past Experiences*

Sometimes, the reason why you are so angry may be because of certain things that you have experienced in the past. If you have been in situations that made you angry in the past, but you had to suppress that anger then because there was no way to express it safely, you may still be nursing those feelings of anger without you knowing this.

Trauma, abuse, and bullying are some of the horrible experiences that could put a person in a perpetual state of anger. Research has shown that people who bully others are usually those who were also bullied by others.

If you are an employer and you are aggressive towards your workers i.e., you bully them, it could be because you were bullied by people in college or high school while growing up. Most of the people who bully others on social media are those that are actually being bullied by others in reality.

People who have been physically, verbally, emotionally, or sexually abused in the past may be angry due to the hurt they feel from being abused. If a person was sexually abused by someone of the opposite sex, this person might be unusually aggressive and angry towards every one of the opposite sex.

Trauma is also another experience that may be the cause of anger. Traumatic experiences usually have lasting effects on a person, even when they think they have moved on from experience. Memories of past trauma can lead to feelings of anxiety, frustration, and hopelessness, which can trigger angry episodes.

Past experiences put you in a situation where you find certain situations unusually challenging, and this leaves you prone to getting angry. Sometimes, your current feelings of anger are not the product of whatever situation you are currently in. Rather, they are linked to past experiences. What this means is that the situation you are presently in reflects something from your past.

To deal with anger, you must first become aware of the particular experience from the past, which is serving as the underlying trigger for anger.

• *Present Circumstances*

There are also times when the factor triggering your anger is the current circumstance you find yourself in. If you have a lot going on in your life presently, you may find yourself more prone to anger than you ever were. You may also be getting angry at totally unconnected things.

Many people get angry easily because they are in a situation that makes them angry, but they don't feel courageous enough to address the situation or resolve it directly.

Let's look at an example. If your boss at work is unusually difficult and aggressive towards you, this will surely make you angry. But, since he is your boss, you may not be bold enough to address the issue with him.

This means you have to bottle the anger in. But the thing about anger is that it can't be repressed for long. So, you may turn the anger towards your colleagues at work or your children at home. Something as trivial as your child spilling water on the floor may trigger angry feelings.

In this case, your situation at work is what is making you angry, but you don't feel like you can actually address it because you don't want to lose your job. This makes you redirect the anger to your colleagues or the poor kids at home.

• *Helplessness or Powerlessness*

This is a common trigger for anger, especially among men. You may be getting angrier than usual because you are in a situation that feels completely out of your control, and you feel helpless. That example of your boss at work comes to mind in this situation.

Powerlessness is often associated with feelings of helplessness and a loss of control over the events in one's life. People like to feel in control, so they get angry when a situation that isn't within their control comes to play.

If you have issues with your health or you are in an abusive relationship that you feel you can't get out of, you may feel intensely angry because of how helpless you are in that situation.

The key here is always to remind yourself that some things will either be within or outside your control. But, there are situations where you are completely in control; it is simply left for you to exercise that control.

• *Stress and Anxiety*

The Anxiety and Depression Association released data that show that more than 40 million American adults suffer from anxiety, and this is almost a whopping 18 percent of the total population of the United States.

Like I already explained, anger, stress, and anxiety are three closely-knitted conditions. People who suffer from anxiety-related conditions often experience overwhelming and out-of-control reactions. They usually end up expressing their stress and frustration in the form of anger.

Often, tensed and uncertain situations may make a person angry due to the pressure they leave on the shoulder and the brain.

• *Grief*

The last common cause of anger, which you should know, is grief. Usually, an overwhelming emotion, grief often comes from painful situations. It is also associated with hardship and loss.

Feelings of grief may arise from the death of a loved one, a pet, or a friend. It may also be induced by professional and career-related situations like the loss of your job.

When grief overwhelms you, it may quickly turn to transform into anger. This anger often arises as a result of the frustration and unfairness felt by the grieving person. For instance, if you lose your spouse, just thinking of the future you both envisioned might leave you feeling frustrated, wronged, and angry at the cruelty and unfairness of your situation.

Your anger may be especially directed at people for not being able to understand how you truly feel or sympathize with your situation and the suffering.

Apart from the ones we just checked out together, there are several other things that may be triggering your anger with you being oblivious to them. In a subsequent chapter, I will explain how you can identify and recognize your anger triggers in order to control your anger.

Chapter Two

Anger as a Positive Emotion

If you think of anger as a wild, uncontrollable, and negative emotion, it is normal because you aren't the only one who thinks this. I can boldly assume that more than half of the world's population, if not more, think of anger as a negative emotion.

This is understandable, considering how society has raised everyone to view anger as an unwanted and abominable emotion. But, as opposed to everything you have learned while growing up, anger can actually be a positive emotion.

In fact, it is safe to say that anger as an emotion is neither positive nor negative. Like I already said, it is simply an emotion. Emotion is bodily responses, and they aren't meant to be negative or positive, in the real sense.

However, certain factors are what influence the decision to tag some emotions as positive, and others are negative. Some of these include the reaction inspired by these emotions, how they affect someone, and the consequence of feeling that emotion.

Therefore, a known 'positive' emotion, such as optimism, may turn out to be negative in some cases, especially in cases where it is over-the-top. In the same breath, an emotion like anger, which is considered by all and sundry to be negative, may turn out to be positive in certain instances. It all depends on how you react to both emotions.

I'm not saying that it is wrong for you or anybody else to view anger as a negative emotion, especially when you consider all the damaging consequences it usually results in. What I am saying is that your interpretation and reaction to anger is what determines whether it becomes a negative or positive emotion. In itself, anger is simply an emotion, a response your body activates when it perceives danger.

Like most people, you probably don't know that anger can be a positive emotion. As you already learned, people often feel angry in situations that are displeasing, unjust, or hostile. This means that anger isn't something that just comes out of nowhere; it surfaces when something that makes you uncomfortable occurs.

So, anger becomes positive when you react to hostile, unfair, or displeasing situations healthily and positively. For example, if someone insults you and you calmly walk away instead of giving a retort, does it mean you weren't angry? No, you simply chose to react to your anger by leaving the environment, which is a positive reaction.

Anger can be a positive emotion in more than one way.

● *Promotes Survival*

Anger is designed to promote human survival. The "fight or flight" response is meant to alert us about danger so we can defend ourselves. Anger is ingrained deeply into humans' primitive need to live and survive against danger or aggression.

Thus, anger gears you to be extra vigilant about threats, and it also improves your focus. When someone or something attacks you, the brain immediately activates anger so you can fight back or flee from the scene of the attack in order to protect yourself.

● *Powerful Motivator*

Firstly, anger can serve as a motivating force when channeled rightly. One of the things I usually tell people with anger problems is to 'channel anger into positive energy,' and I'm sure you may have heard this from other people too.

Anger, in itself, is positive energy, which can also serve as a motivating force when used right. Several research has shown that anger can push people towards their goals, despite problems, barriers, and obstructions.

When you see something you really want, and you feel angry because you aren't getting that thing, the anger you feel may become a powerful motivator that pushes you to work harder in order to get that thing.

Anger provides you with a sense of power and control that makes it much easier for you to press on and get what you want.

• *Optimism*

This probably feels strange to your sight and odd to your ears, but anger makes people more optimistic. This is one thing angry people have in common with happy people; they are both characteristically more optimistic than other people. This is a fact backed up with evidence from research.

The optimism you feel from being angry is what sometimes motivates you to press harder towards your goals without giving up, no matter how many barriers or problems you face on the way.

Anger gives you hope and makes you feel like anything is achievable. For example: if you write a test in school and you score an 'F,' you may become angry as a result of this. This anger could, in turn, make you work harder on your next test and leave you optimistic that you won't be failing again.

• *Improve Relationships*

Anger is used to communicate a sense of wrong and injustice as a natural reaction. But, society tells you anger is destructive, harmful, and you should never let it show. This proves to be largely negative on your relationships.

Interestingly enough, research has also shown that hiding your anger in a relationship affects the health of that relationship. The thing is, when you suppress or hide anger, you are making it impossible for your partner to know that they have done something to offend or wrong you.

So, they may perpetuate that particular behavior, making you angry, and this can be detrimental to the relationship.

But, when communicated and expressed healthily, anger actually benefits a relationship. If your partner does something that makes you angry and you immediately let them know, they apologize, and you both work towards a solution to prevent the ugly situation from occurring again.

This turns out to be healthier and of more benefit to your relationship; it strengthens the bond in the relationship. Sometimes, the lack of effective communication is what leads to so much anger and conflicts in a relationship.

When channeled positively, anger can prove to be of tremendous benefit to your personal and professional relationships.

● *Provides Insight*

When you channel it the right way, anger gives you useful insight into yourself. In some cases, angry outbursts often end up, resulting in positive outcomes. This is because it provides you with insight into your own faults.

The fact that you are currently reading this book is also proof that anger really provides insight. You are probably reading this book because you have looked inwards and realized that there is something wrong with you that needs to be addressed and corrected as soon as possible.

Knowing when you get angry, why you get angry, and what makes you angry can impact and improve your life in a number of positive ways. Just as it motivates you to work harder towards accomplishing your goals, anger can also motivate self-change by inspiring you to seek out what aspect of yourself or your life needs to be addressed, corrected, and improved

● *Reduces Violence*

I know this may seem like a completely ludicrous thing to say, especially when you consider the fact that violence is mostly always preceded by anger. But, I promise you that anger can also be channeled to reduce violence.

This is because anger is a very strong emotion that points you to the fact that something exists to be resolved. Usually, when people know that they have done something to make you angry, and they also notice the signals in your countenance, they are more driven to placate you and diffuse the situation.

If you are still unsure about the plausibility of anger being a way to reduce violence, take a moment, and imagine a world where no one gets angry. Imagine a world where no one has any method of showing their displeasure about an injustice. In a world like this, isn't it possible that people may just proceed straight to violence since there is no means of letting others know how they feel.

- *Negotiation*

Anger is an emotion that you can use legitimately and strategically to get something you want. In a certain study that was conducted in 2002, it was observed that people made fewer demands of an angry person, particularly in relation to a job or project.

This provides evidence that you can use anger to facilitate the negotiation, but this process is a little complicated. The best time to use anger as a negotiation strategy is when it is justified.

If you use anger legitimately and strategically to get something you really want, you are channeling anger as a positive emotion.

- *Release Tension*

Anger makes you experience physical and emotional pain. In that state of distress, anger strongly pushes you to correct the situation. Therefore, anger helps to manage stress in the body by serving as an outlet for releasing tension, thereby calming your nerves.

This explains why people usually feel calm right after having an angry reaction.

- *Improves Emotional Intelligence*

People who are comfortable with accepting and embracing seemingly uncomfortable emotions like anger, instead of suppressing or avoiding them, are usually very emotionally intelligent.

Emotionally intelligent people don't avoid, fight, or resist anger. Instead, they embrace it and channel it into becoming more productive. This makes them more resilient and adaptive in challenging situations.

You will learn more about how to develop and enhance your emotional intelligence as you read further. Emotional intelligence and anger/stress management actually go hand-in-hand because you can't manage your emotions if you aren't even aware of these emotions.

Despite the strongly negative reputation of anger, more and more people are starting to accept the reality of anger as a constructive and positive emotion when channeled right, including all the benefits it could add to their lives.

Anger is a core part of the "fight or flight" response, and this makes it very much natural. It is crucial to your existence and survival. When channeled right, anger has a positive impact on a person.

But, anger becomes negative and destructive when it becomes overwhelming and out-of-control. Anger is meant to give you a sense of control over life, not take control of your life.

Anger as a Negative Emotion

When anger isn't being productive, it means it isn't positive. Destructive anger i.e., anger, which has a lot of damaging consequences, is what is regarded as negative anger.

Sadly, the negative aspect of anger seems to outweigh the positives because many people allow themselves to be overwhelmed by anger.

Anger becomes negative when you aren't channeling it productively, and it is affecting more than one area of your life, including your personal, social, and professional relationships. Uncontrollable anger can have devastating effects on you and the people who are closest to you.

It is what normally results in physical abuse, violence, conflict, assault, and even self-harm. In the most extreme form, anger can lead to something as terrifying as murder. Unlike positive anger, negative anger destroys your life in so many ways, which include;

● *Health*

One of the areas where negative anger majorly affects your life is your health. When you hear people say you are doing yourself more harm by being angry, you should accept that as the truth because even science has backed it up with substantial proof.

Whether you express it explosively, suppress it or, turn it inwards to yourself, anger can wreak havoc on your health. Chronic anger has been associated with an increased risk of certain health issues.

The duration, intensity, and frequency of anger are some of the major determinants of how it affects and impacts your health.

Anger has been linked to many heart-related problems. Explosive angry outbursts place your cardiac health at great risk. According to experts, the possibility of having a heart attack doubles within two hours of experiencing an explosive anger episode.

Repressed anger has also been linked with a number of heart diseases. A study provides proof that people who are uncontrollably prone to anger are more susceptible to the risk of having a coronary disease than people who experience anger less.

Another study has also shown that anger puts you at an increased risk of suffering a stroke. According to the study, an individual is thrice at a higher risk of suffering a stroke from bleeding within the brain, usually within the two hours after an anger episode. People with an aneurysm in any of the brain arteries are at six times risk in the event of an angry outburst.

Anger also weakens the immune system. If you are the type who is ever angry, then you may find yourself getting sick more often than usual. In fact, just recalling an experience from the past that makes you angry causes a six-hour drop in your body's level of immunoglobulin, an antibody which is your body's first defense against an invasion of infection.

That's not all, though; negative anger increases anxiety and is also linked to depressive disorders. Several studies have established a strong connection between depression and explosive anger, especially in men. Passive anger is especially prominent in people with depressive disorders.

You may not smoke, but your lung is still at great risk if you let yourself get mad all the time. This fact is backed up by the results of a study conducted by scientists of the Harvard Medical School.

• *Self-esteem*

In the spur of the moment, the expression of negative anger often leaves a person feeling powerful and good. You know that "Yeah, I dealt with his silly ass by punching his silly head in" feeling after you have just dealt with someone who insulted you and woke the raging tiger in you.

Negative anger may make you feel good at the moment, but it usually results in feelings of shame, guilt, embarrassment, and remorse, all of which are not comfortable in the least. Cognitively, you may realize that your reaction was blown completely out of proportion, misdirected, or even unwarranted. This could lead to a dent in your self-esteem.

You may start avoiding the person you reacted angrily towards or social situations as a whole because you are scared of letting that kind of situation repeat itself. The angrier you are, the more damage you do to your self-esteem.

Naturally, a need to feel empathy and compassion for others is embedded in us all as humans. So, when we act in a way that counters that need, it leaves a major impact on our self-esteem.

In a way, when you suppress your anger without paying attention to whatever it is trying to alert you to, it could also affect your self-esteem. If you are the type who thinks it is okay to accept whatever people throw at you, you might be unable to set appropriate boundaries.

With the lack of necessary boundaries to tell people off when necessary, you are basically walking around with a "walk around on me the way you like" tag. What usually happens here is that internal pressure builds up the more you suppress anger until it gets to a point where you can no longer hold the anger in, and it erupts in a massive explosion. Then, you feel shame, guilt, and remorse, which takes a dip on your self-esteem.

Some people neither express their anger unhealthily nor suppress it, they turn it inwards instead. If you are the type who does this, you are subconsciously shaming yourself. The way this works is that something dissatisfying or disappointing happens in the environment, but instead of addressing this thing directly, you conclude that it is your fault and become angry with yourself.

This makes you find faults with yourself without feeling disconnected from the other person. In your mind, you were completely responsible for the situation, and the other party didn't do anything wrong. Something like this mostly happens with victims of abuse and assault.

Soon, you may start to breed contempt for yourself just because of your inability to control your feelings of anger.

● *Relationships*

One of the most common damages to relationships is an inability to manage one's anger. In fact, it is probably on the list of things that are quick to end a relationship. No one wants to be friends or anything with a person who can't manage their anger.

Just as laughter is contagious, emotions like anger are also contagious. When expressed or channeled negatively, anger doesn't only affect you, but it also affects people around you. Anger casts a negative shadow on the relationship you have with the people closest to you.

In the mildest instance, anger may make people become upset, intimidated, scared, or put off by you. Negative anger puts you at the risk of pushing important people out of your life forever.

Negative anger makes you vent or lash out at your partner, verbally or physically, and this could have a major negative effect on the person's wellbeing. Screaming, yelling, shoving, or pushing your partner may seem like minor things when you are in the heat of anger.

But, they can lead to major destructive consequences, which can be devastating to your partner's health, causing them to sever the relationship they have with you.

Apart from your personal relationships, anger can also affect your professional relationships. You may find yourself being fired from different workplaces consecutively just because you are unnecessarily aggressive towards your colleagues at work.

Your level of productivity in the workplace, both qualitatively and quantitatively, can be poorly impacted by uncontrollable anger, resentment, and frustration.

Uncontrollable anger can have adverse effects on your health, relationships, self-esteem, and productivity if you don't check it immediately. Remember that I said anger in itself is neither positive nor negative, but you can determine if your anger is positive/productive or negative/destructive based on how you react to it and the aftermaths of that anger.

If you look within yourself and recognize that your anger is more destructive than positive, it is time to learn how to channel anger into more positive and productive things, which could be of benefits to you and the people around you. It means anger management is more to you crucial now than it ever was.

Is Anger Good or Bad?

In very candid terms, anger is a very problematic emotion (if not the most problematic emotion). The fact that people find it difficult to control anger is one of the reasons why it is considered a problematic emotion.

But, does being problematic mean anger is a bad emotion? In fact, I often meet people who want to know if anger is a good or bad emotion. Of course, the answer I usually give is that anger is neither a bad or good emotion, just as it isn't a negative or positive emotion.

As I already posited, anger isn't primarily negative or positive emotion, so you can't say it is bad, or it is good.

What determines whether anger is good or bad is how you handle it, and the way you put it to use, whether the outcome is positive or not. If you see a person being harassed on the streets and you get angry, then this anger is good.

If you observe someone doing something extremely harmful to you behind your back and you get angry, this anger is also good. If you get angry at an injustice that has been committed against someone in the society and you feel angry, this anger is good.

Anger may be considered good when it is being induced by a situation that spells injustice or hostility. Anger is usually a good emotion when it is primary, coming from a place of hurt that makes you want to do something.

I have observed something quite common with anger: people with anger problems are mostly always masking another emotion with that anger just because they don't feel courageous enough to express that particular emotion. This usually makes it 'bad' and negative.

But, when anger is direct, primary, and purely unadulterated without any feeling hiding behind it, it usually comes from a good place. You are simply just trying to protect yourself or somebody else.

There are different types of anger, which you will learn about soon. The type of anger you are experiencing is what usually determines whether your anger is good or bad anger. Anger such as justified anger may be considered good since it is due to a situation where you were wronged, but passive-aggressive anger may not qualify as good anger because of how it is being handled.

Therefore, the only way to determine if your anger is good or bad is to identify the cause, recognize how it is being handled, and embrace where it is coming from. In itself, anger is neither bad/negative or good/positive.

How to Channel Anger Positively and Productively

The key to gaining control over your anger and let it stop controlling your life is to start channeling the anger proactively into more positive and productive things. The problem is many people have no idea how to channel anger positively in order to improve their lives.

The foundation to channeling anger productively is to start sieving out the negative things and concentrate wholly on the positive things, no matter how little or inconsequential they seem. You probably don't believe this, but the little things actually matter.

No matter what you face or the challenges before you, it is vital to always put yourself in a position where you see nothing but the positive aspects of every situation you find yourself in. For example: if you receive a notice from work that your employer will be laying off some workers, you may naturally start to feel scared, and this fear may become angry at your employers.

Rather than letting yourself get trapped in a cycle of anxiety and anger because of what is about to happen at work, you can choose that period to reevaluate your skill sets, strengths, and weaknesses and channel that anger into an energy directed at preparing yourself in the eventuality that you need to get a new job.

Another example: let's assume that you have been abused severally by different people growing up. Of course, this will make you undoubtedly angry. But instead of being angry at yourself and concentrating on the unfortunate situation in which you found yourself, you can instead focus on the fact that there are thousands of people in the exact situation as yours and then devise means through which you can help them and inadvertently help yourself too.

In a situation like this, you are pushing yourself to see beyond the woes of your situation and focus on the opportunities that lie underneath.

Anger can also be channeled productively into more positive aspects of your life by getting rid of limiting beliefs and thoughts. As I already said, negative thinking patterns are some of the causes of negative anger patterns in some people.

Sometimes, the negative perspective you have of yourself is what is breeding the negative emotions beneath your anger. When you talk or think badly of yourself, you start to believe and accept your thoughts as the truth.

Instead of letting negative thoughts and beliefs become an integral part of your self-image and value system, replace them immediately with positive and self-evaluating thoughts. For instance, if you catch yourself thinking something like "I'm such a horrible person," immediately replace that thought with something like, "I'm a great person."

Instantly, your brain will process the positive thought and respond accordingly. This may seem like an oddly silly thing to do at first, but you will be surprised at how fast your brain is at manifesting positive affirmations and thoughts.

Intriguingly, the brain can only think one thing at a time. So, when you replace negative thoughts with positive ones, it means your brain can only concentrate on the positive thought at that moment. The power of positive thinking is actually a thing because positive thoughts breed positive emotions.

To start using anger to engage in more productive things, and facilitate positive outcomes, follow the steps below.

• *Channel It*

Of course, this is what we have been talking about, right? The first, simple, and most straightforward way to productively utilize anger is to direct it to a task –any task that can keep the thought of making your angry from your mind.

Channeling your anger is quite wise because it not only helps you avoid getting in a situation, you are likely to regret the aftermath, it also makes it possible for you to use anger to attend to more important tasks at that moment.

When channeling your anger, ensure that it is towards something positive. Have you ever been in a situation where someone annoyed you, and you choose that moment to stomp off to the kitchen and do the dishes? This is a classic example of channeling your anger towards a task.

Whenever you find yourself getting angry, choose that moment to complete a project you have been putting off for long; take out your bicycle and do a quick one down the road; start cleaning meticulously around the house, or use that time to respond to the hundreds of emails you left unread in your inbox.

One thing you will come to understand is that productivity knows no bound when you are angry. Directing your anger to a task when you are angry could open your eyes to some talents you didn't even know you had.

• *Plan*

I already said that anger could be a very strong motivating force when used right, so why not choose that moment you are feeling angry to make some crucial plans. The thing with angry people is that they are also usually determined, more than other people.

Therefore, it only makes sense to use that determination to plan something that could be really beneficial to your life. Turn your anger around into a 2-year plan aimed at improving your career or improving yourself a human.

Anger is an energy that is meant to be put to use, so don't let that energy waste away or spiral into something that could later affect your life. Make a plan!

● *Execute the plan*

One of the best periods to execute a plan is when you are still feeling that surge of motivation and optimism that comes with being angry. As soon as you create a plan, executing the steps contained within becomes much easier.

Use that energy that comes from being angry to pursue everything contained in your plan before that anger/energy wears off. Riding off the wave of rage can be of tremendous advantage to an individual, even if they don't know it.

Look at an instance. In most of the revenge-centered movies you have watched, there is always someone who has been wronged, and this person usually feels anger to a point where they conceive a master plan and proceed to take steps to ensure the success of this plan so as to achieve the revenge they seek.

Now, I'm not saying that you should let anger push you to revenge too. I'm simply illustrating how anger can be a perfect motivation for executing any plan you have got.

• *Don't think or doubt*

After you create a plan and strategically analyze your moves, actions, and everything, it is normal to start feeling doubtful and pensive and end up in the cesspool of your anger. The best thing to do in this situation is to execute without thinking.

If you let yourself ruminate too much over the plan, you may get caught up in your mind and thinking processes. What you should do is go ahead with the execution of your plan. By eliminating space for reflection, it becomes impossible for you to doubt your abilities or question the plan you have.

• *Crosscheck*

Making a plan with anger makes it quite easy to make high-end mistakes that may come to bite. The right thing to do is to crosscheck or double-check your plan so as to ensure there are no mistakes that could be costly.

Ensure the adrenaline-driven energy you used in creating the plan hasn't made you make mistakes that you ordinarily wouldn't. Don't let anger consume you to the point where you can't objectively assess your plan before you execute it.

• *Monitor your progress*

Even with a plan and everything, it is easy to lose yourself and let anger bring out the worst in you. Therefore, ensure you always monitor yourself in order to know your progress. Assess your plan and know the kind of emotions it is eliciting in you.

Know how that emotion is influencing whatever approach you are taking towards the achievement of your plan. Also, recognize the effect it has on the people around you, especially those closest to you.

Conclusively, it is important to make sure that you stay within your limit in whatever you do. Every human has a personal speed limit, and it is vital that you know and acknowledge your personal speed limit.

Knowledge of your personal speed limit makes it impossible for you to keep a situation from escalating beyond your control while sticking perfectly to the content of your plan and the goals/objectives.

Chapter Three

Types of Anger

Just as it is important to know the cause of your anger and the source fueling that emotion, it is also very important for you to know the type of anger you feel in different situations. I usually tell people that knowing the type of anger you are experiencing is the start of controlling that anger.

Why do I say this? Because it lets you know how best to react to that anger. Different types of anger are meant to be reacted to in a different way, and once you know that, it becomes easy to master the right reaction to particular anger.

The type of anger you experience is measured by certain factors, the most relevant in the context of the situation that caused that anger. Often, I meet people who mistake anger types and anger communication styles, but they are not the same.

Types of anger are basically categorized by the context surrounding the emotion, while anger communication style refers to how a person expresses anger. Of course, I'll also talk about anger communication styles along the way.

Justifiable Anger

The first type of anger I want you to know is the justifiable anger. This is the kind of anger that fuels the Martin Luther Kings of this world in order to fight against injustice. Justifiable anger comes from feeling a sense of moral outrage at injustice, wrongs, and inequality.

People who fight against things such as human oppression or domestic violence do so because of the anger they feel at the situation. Usually, justifiable anger is healthy, important, and beneficial because it gives you the motivation to right a wrong.

The intensity with which it comes can become a passion and be channeled as a tool for change or accomplishment of certain goals, in the short term.

However, in the long run, it could become unhealthy by turning into an obsession and stealing away your peace of mind. Justifiable anger causes turmoil and suffering when it becomes obsessive.

It doesn't matter whether the anger is over an injustice, unfairness, or anything else. When you stay angry on a regular basis, you will only cause hurt to yourself in the long run. The best way to handle justifiable anger is to channel it as a tool for inspiring change, especially in regards to the situation causing the anger.

Judgmental Anger

This is another quite common type of anger that seems to be rampant amongst a lot of people. Judgmental anger could be good anger, depending on the context. It is quite similar to justifiable anger, and many people actually interchange both.

But, there is a distinct difference. Although both anger usually originates from a place of moral, judgmental anger has more to do with perceived slights on one's personal beliefs or values.

If someone does things in a way that you think isn't appropriate and you get angry, that is judgmental anger. It doesn't matter that this thing may not be wrong in the general and widely acceptable perception of wrong.

As long as it isn't something that conforms to your personal beliefs or values, you are bound to get angry. For instance, people who get angry because of other people's personal choices do so from a place of judgment.

It comes from you assuming a morally superior stance in a situation and getting angry when another person falls below your moral expectations. It is anger fueled by other people's shortcomings.

When expressed excessively, judgmental anger could alienate you from family, friends, and prospective allies. The best way to manage or handle judgmental anger is to always explore other perspectives in any situation you are. This provides insights in a meaningful way.

Annoyance Anger

When you think of anger that originates from very petty or little things, that is what annoyance anger is. It is the most common type of anger- the type we all experience. Annoyance anger usually originates from the many frustrations and stressors of daily life.

It is that anger you feel from having to spend a whole day with your jerk of a boss at work, struggling to get your kids to listen to you, getting into an argument with your partner, and so on. The list of things that cause annoyance anger can go on and on.

This type of anger can also arise from your inability to externalize people's words, opinions, and actions towards you. When you find it impossible to make yourself unaffected by what other people say or do, you leave yourself very vulnerable to anger.

Focusing on the negatives is one reason why so many people experience annoyance anger so much. One thing you should always know as a human being is that people will always have good or bad to say about you, no matter how hard you try to mold their opinions of you.

So, the best thing is to take everything in stride and never take things personally. What other people say and do to you can simply be regarded as a projection of their forced reality.

Overwhelming Anger

This is uncontrollable anger at its best; it always gets the best of you no matter how hard you try to curtail it. Overwhelming anger is that kind of anger you never seem capable of controlling. You just always find yourself losing it, even when you try not to.

Overwhelming anger usually arises as a result of frustration, hopelessness, and helplessness. It occurs as a result of the loss of your sense of control over life and whatever situation you find yourself.

It often originates when you have too much responsibility or when life throws itself hard at you unexpectedly. It also occurs when you are no longer able to cope with feelings of stress and anxiety.

Grief and trauma are some of the core sources of overwhelming anger. Usually, you may find yourself unable to identify the source of your anger despite trying really hard. You simply find yourself giving in to anger and unable to curtail the response.

When experiencing overwhelming anger, the ideal thing is to find someone to talk it over with. Whatever you are feeling, ensure you talk to someone close or a professional therapist about it. Healthy, verbal communication is usually the best outlet for overwhelming anger. It gives a sense of direction and control, which is lacking.

Chronic Anger

Anger becomes chronic when it becomes continual, ultimately destructive, devastating, affective, and never-ending. Chronic anger is the worst because it affects your health and wellbeing in ways you can't even begin to imagine.

It is usually generalized, with feelings of resentment, annoyance, and displeasure towards others even without a plausible reason. It is also anger towards yourself; chronic anger is both internalized and externalized, depending on the situation or cause.

Rather than just being an emotion, chronic anger often becomes a habit. It becomes a part of you that can't be shaken off, no matter what. Habitual irritation, annoyance, disgust, and displeasure at the slightest things and even seemingly happy situations.

Chronic anger is usually prolonged, making it have an adverse effect on physical, psychological, and emotional health and wellbeing. It usually requires professional help.

Volatile Anger

Quite similar to chronic anger in terms of how badly it affects you, volatile anger is the explosive type of anger that always originates out of nowhere. This is already obvious from the word "volatile," which means "prone to sudden change or violence."

You never know when it hits you. Most times, you just find yourself getting angry at the slightest impulses, even when the cause of annoyance is trivial. The amusing thing is you find yourself calming down just as quickly as you exploded when it comes to volatile anger.

Managing volatile anger starts with mastering the signs and physiological symptoms, which precede a potentially volatile situation and learning to identify them. Then, you use quick relaxation techniques to subside the anger whenever you feel it rising.

Next, let's check out the anger communication styles. Both anger types and communication styles are not mutually exclusive because they impact each other in a way.

Anger Communication Styles

Everyone has a communication style unique to them. The communication style doesn't have to do with anger only, but for the purpose of this book, I will be talking specifically about common anger communication styles in human beings.

Anger communication style refers to how you express feelings of anger whenever you are experiencing the emotion. Keep it in mind that a person can have different communication styles for anger, depending on the cause and context of the situation, feeling that anger.

It is important to know the different anger communication styles because it provides insight that lets you know when you are angry. Some anger communication styles are so subtle that you won't even know that it is anger you are experiencing.

So, once you know and have the means to recognize all, it becomes easier to manage the anger and control the emotions and behavior it elicits. I'll be talking about five anger communication styles, which are;

- Assertive anger style
- Aggressive anger style

- Passive anger style

- Passive-aggressive anger style

- Projective-aggressive style

Assertive Anger Style

Experts have attested that this is the most constructive style of anger communication, and there are so many things to complement this submission. Assertive communication style is when frustration, anger, and rage push you to facilitate positive change.

People with an assertive communication style express anger by vying for necessary changes in their lives or around the world, rather than internalizing or expressing the anger verbally, physically, or violently.

The best thing about assertive anger is that it is communicated without any form of distress or destructive behavior. Therefore, it is the best and healthiest way for you to express anger without causing harm to yourself or the people around you.

You may use assertiveness as a tool for motivation and also use it to address underlying feelings behind your anger. Assertiveness makes it quite easy to deal with injustice and also accomplish whatever you set your mind to in life.

Aggressive Anger Style

The aggressive communication style of anger is the type that violence accompanies. Anger, which is expressed aggressively, always comes with hostility and force. Usually, people with aggressive communication styles have a need to be in control of certain situations, other people, and themselves.

This is expressed through manipulation and blame-shifting. Aggressive people never take no for an answer. They always find ways to make other people submit to their gimmicks by guilt-tripping them.

This style of anger communication is understandably destructive because it mostly always results in violence. Aggressiveness often results in emotional, physical, and verbal abuse for subjects of anger.

But, the effects are usually more devastating for the person experiencing that anger than for people who are the subject of the anger. The best way to manage this communication style is to hone your emotional intelligence skills and also master control over your emotions. It's really straightforward.

Passive Anger Style

Passive communication of anger has to do with internalizing anger, without ever expressing it outwards for others to see. This particular anger communication style is quite dangerous because it hurts your wellbeing in the long run.

People who communicate anger passively have a knack for always putting others first without ever considering their own feelings, thoughts, and needs. A typical passive communicator will rather not let a person know when he or she is angry in order to avoid upsetting the other party.

Humans tend to walk all over people who never express how they feel because they see them as easy targets. This fuels the anger even more because no one wants to be a walk-over, obviously. It often leads to a buildup of resentment and dissatisfaction.

Passive anger can be really damaging to you. It hurts your self-esteem, confidence, and more importantly, your health and wellbeing. The right thing for a passive communicator to do is to learn and master how to become confident and assertive in communicating your thoughts, feelings, and opinions.

Passive-aggressive Anger Style

Passive-aggressiveness is a quite common communication style among many people. In fact, most people don't even know it is anger being expressed when they are passive-aggressive. This is because it is an avoidant communication style.

People act passive-aggressively out of a need to communicate their feelings while evading possible confrontations, arguments, or fights. If you are a passive-aggressive person, it means you always repress and deny any feelings of frustration, displeasure, or anger so as to avoid getting into a fight.

Normally, this kind of anger is communicated through other means such as veiled mockery, sarcasm, pointed silence, and even verbally.

Sometimes, it is also expressed physically i.e., a person intentionally indulges chronic procrastination.

The interesting thing about passive-aggressiveness is that you think you are communicating your anger passively without knowing it is actually being perceived or received as aggressive. A passive-aggressive communication style usually has adverse effects on the relationships you share with others, whether personal or professional.

Projective-aggressive anger style

Finally, we have the projective-aggressive anger communication style, which most people tend to confuse with passive anger style.

A projective-aggressive person is usually scared to own up to their anger or express it. So, they instead project feelings of anger and other related emotions onto others in order to get them to act out or express their anger for them.

For instance, if you are a person with a projective-aggressive anger style and you get into an anger-inducing argument, which of course makes you angry with another person, you may say to this person that they look angry even when they don't appear so.

In reality, this is just you trying to project your anger on this person so that they may express it instead. In normal situations, telling a person, they appear angry in the midst of a hostile argument may actually make them angry.

Of course, there are other styles of communicating anger, but many people prefer to classify these as types of anger rather than styles of anger communication. They include;

- Behavioral anger: This may also be referred to as physical anger because it is often expressed physically with the use of aggression.

- Retaliatory anger: If you find yourself always vying for revenge or retaliation when someone offends you, then that is you expressing your anger by getting back at whoever offends you.

- Self-abusive anger: This is also a way of expressing anger through internalization. For instance, you may result in the use of drugs and substances just to let others know you are angry. But, you are just causing harm to yourself.

- Verbal anger: Usually expressed through insults, sarcasm, etc. verbal anger is the perfect example of passive-aggressive anger.

One of the reasons why it is important that you learn the different anger communication styles is so that you can avoid the mistake of confusing one for another.

This brings me to the issue of anger and aggression. It is almost impossible to talk about anger or anger styles without giving a mention to aggression. Unfortunately, many people often confuse anger for aggression because of how closely related both reactions are.

So, let me get you enlightened on what exactly the difference (s) between anger and aggression are! You will find it an interesting read.

Anger and Aggression: What is the Difference?

To start with, I have met so many people who always say things like, "Oh, an angry person is also an aggressive person," or "You can't be angry without being aggressive." First of all, you can be angry without being aggressive, but you can't be aggressive without being angry because aggression stems from anger.

The first thing I always say to anyone who juxtaposes anger and aggression for each other is that anger is an emotion, while aggression is a behavior. It really is as simple as that.

Anger is something you feel, while aggression is something you act out. You are aggressive when you express your anger physically. You should also know that anger is the root of aggression, so if you are aggressive, it means there are deep feelings of anger or some primary emotions underlying that particular behavior.

There are plenty of differences between anger and aggression. To start with, anger is a normal and natural emotion, while aggression is not normal. It isn't something everyone experiences; it originates from a place of hurt and pain.

Everybody feels angry once in a while, even the calmest people. However, people try to deny feelings of anger because of the stigma associated with anger. The idea is that anyone who gets angry is a 'bad' person, but as I already said, anger is a subjective emotion.

While anger is a normal physiological reaction to threat or perceived danger, aggression is a choice; something you choose to do. The fact that you are feeling angry gives you no ground to become violent towards others, but some people choose to behave like this.

Aggression is a behavior that many people choose to exhibit, consciously. Out of anger, aggressive people try to bully others into succumbing to their needs, even if they don't want to. When you act aggressively, you aren't acknowledging the other party's needs, you are bullying them into accepting yours.

Another thing is that anger isn't a problem like most people like to think, but aggression is. Yes, anger could be a problem, but in the primary nature, it is not a problem. It only becomes a problem when you act it out aggressively or passive-aggressively.

As a necessary emotion, anger is acceptable, but aggression isn't because it is a problem, and it needs to be managed. Anger becomes a problem when you start exhibiting aggressive behaviors because of it. The aggressive tendencies that come with anger are what makes it a potential problem.

Aggression plays out in two ways: instrumental aggression and receptive aggression. In the case of instrumental aggression, the aim is not to cause harm to the object of the anger, but it could be a consequence.

On the other hand, receptive aggression or responsive aggression, as it is also called, has the specific objective of causing harm with intent. This kind of aggression depicts hostility at the peak.

Again, anger is a temporary physiological and emotional state resulting from hurt, pain, disappointment, and frustration. But, aggression is a regular behavioral problem, something that happens every time. It is a constant and regular attempt at causing harm to another person or property.

Conclusively, what I want you to take away from this is that anger and aggression are two different things, even if we sometimes tend to mistake them for each other. An angry person may be aggressive, but an aggressive person is in a state of perpetual or continual anger.

Anger as a Secondary Emotion

I said from the first anger is most times a secondary emotion even though it is often regarded as a primary emotion. The truth of this is that most times, there is always an underlying emotion beneath feelings of anger. You don't just experience anger; you experience anger because of some other primary emotion such as fear, sadness, and pain.

Humans often resort to protecting themselves from painful or hurtful emotions by disguising it with anger. This is in order to avoid feeling vulnerable. Anger is often regarded as a strong and powerful emotion, which makes it easy for people, especially men, to express it more.

Primary emotions are those feelings you experience instantaneously in situations, which could elicit them. They are often felt immediately, and the physiological reactions are also immediate.

Because anger is one of the easiest emotions to express, many people always assume that it is primary since it always happens very quickly. However, anger is secondary because we mostly always feel something before we feel angry.

For example, you might feel afraid, offended, frustrated, pressured, attacked, or disrespected. Thus, if any of these emotions come with a certain degree of intensity, it results in feelings of anger, or you mistake it as anger.

Let's say someone insults you and criticizes your work destructively. Of course, you would react angrily in a situation like this, even if you don't express the anger outwardly. In this kind of situation, do you think it is really anger you are feeling?

Yes, you might be feeling angry because of that situation, but your anger is just a resultant emotion. Firstly, you must have felt something before you felt that anger. For instance, you might have felt ashamed, embarrassed, or disrespected.

Then, you experience this primary feeling in the form of anger because you probably consider it to be weak or vulnerable. In this case, anger is a secondary emotion, and shame is the primary emotion.

Know that you must feel any particular emotion first before you can experience anger. The primary emotion usually identified to be behind is fear. This is understandable because the body's "fight or flight response," which is activated when experiencing fear is also enabled in anger.

When you find yourself being constantly angry at everything and everyone, it means that there is a certain thing beneath your anger, hiding, so you never experience it. This may because you think the emotion is too painful, weak, or shameful to express.

One thing I like to say is that anger can be both primary and secondary, although it is usually more of a secondary emotion than a primary one. Anger may be primary in the sense that it all depends on the context of the anger.

For example, if there is a situation where you come across someone being abused or assaulted on the streets, the likely primary emotion you would feel at that kind of situation is pure, raging anger.

Of course, this is a case of injustice, and it would no doubt make you displeased, but the thing here is that injustice isn't an emotion in itself. In this scenario, what you get is an instant feeling of annoyance, irritation, or rage, which all constitute what we call anger.

One reason why I think anger usually turns out to be a substitute emotion for so many people is that they find the primary emotions uncomfortable. No doubt, no one would want to express a feeling they are very uncomfortable with.

There are many factors that could be responsible for this reason I just talked about. The first is that primary emotions like fear, shame, anxiety, jealousy, and envy make a person feel vulnerable; they also make you feel like you aren't in control of the situation.

Therefore, they turn to express anger, which is stronger, powerful, and way easier to control. In fact, anger gives a feeling of control, which many emotions don't give.

Going back to that example of being insulted, the shameful feelings may switch subconsciously to anger without you even knowing it. Therefore, it means you are using anger as a secondary tool to avoid being vulnerable due to shame.

Let's look at another example. If you know a couple that constantly gets into arguments and fights, it may seem like there are serious feelings of anger involved in the conflicts. But, more importantly, there is some underlying feeling of fear.

One of the couples may be scared of being abandoned, and this may lead to paranoia, which serves as the basis for drama and arguments.

In a relationship like that, the fear of abandonment is what fuels the anger. Therefore, it is the primary emotion, while anger is secondary.

Men are usually the ones who express or experience anger as a secondary emotion mostly because of the gender-centric belief that men aren't supposed to express weak feelings such as envy, jealousy, shame, and others.

In a subsequent chapter, I will touch more on how gender affects the experience and response to anger in men and women.

One last thing I want you to know is that most people like to think of anger as a primary emotion because of how reactive it is. There is probably no emotion as reactive as anger because the physiological reactions always come instantly.

In many situations, you will find that your brain hasn't even finished identifying the primary emotion before it automatically switches it to anger. So, many people end up believing that anger is really what they are feeling.

As I said, there are different emotions that could be behind your anger. Some of the most acknowledged primary feelings behind anger include;

- Fear: The most recognized feeling behind anger. When you perceive danger or threat, which elicits fear, you may react with anger rather than anxiety, depending on the situation.

- Pain: Feelings of hurt, rejection, abandonment, criticism, etc. may all manifest as anger so as to serve as a defensive or protective mechanism.

- Frustration: This is a common feeling, usually behind anger. It arises when your self-expectations or expectations of others aren't being met, and you feel yourself getting tired. You may disguise the tiredness as anger.

- Injustice: Finally, people tend to become angry due to a violation of their moral code or the sense of wrong and right.

The best way to be able to tell the emotion underneath your anger whenever you feel yourself getting angry is to hone and develop your sense of self-awareness. Self-awareness means being aware of everything going on with you emotionally, psychologically, or physiologically so you can identify the signs of anger before it comes barging uninvited.

Chapter Four

Culture and Anger

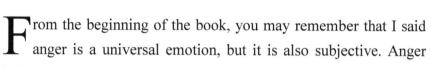

From the beginning of the book, you may remember that I said anger is a universal emotion, but it is also subjective. Anger being subjective means that something that gets you angry may not do the same to another person at all.

One of the reasons why anger is such a subjective emotion is culture. Of course, it is normal to think of anger and other emotions as being universal since every human experience them. However, the difference here is that certain factors often influence how you experience and react to anger.

Culture is a major factor that influences emotional reactions and responses to anger. Another major factor is gender, which is also a product of cultural influences, by the way.

Several studies have provided enough evidence to show that everyone does not react to emotions, including anger, the same way universally. The way you react to emotions is dependent on the culture you were raised in.

The cause of anger, the intensity, the duration, and the anger communication style you use are all influenced by the culture you come from. How society views and judges certain emotions as bad or good is what affects us and the reactions we give to these emotions.

For a long time and after many studies, researchers have uncovered evidence to show that the way anger is expressed in European or western cultures is linked to increased health risks. Interestingly, research also shows that Asian cultures and some others tend to express anger in a way that promotes health and wellbeing.

This means that anger isn't always associated with increased risks of health, except this is influenced by culture. Therefore, while anger may make an American man sick, it may, in fact, improve the health of a person from Japan.

Anger and culture interact in so many ways. Your culture is what determines how you interpret negative thoughts and events. And, like you already know, your expression and reaction to emotion are determined by your interpretation of negative thoughts and events.

Also, culture is the judge of emotional reactions, so it may alter how you perceive yourself, other people, and the world at large.

The Association for Psychological Science published a study recently. According to this study, the implications of anger doesn't come from anger itself but from the circumstances that provoke the anger.

In the United States and other western countries, how you express anger is influenced by how you experience negative events. But in a place like Japan or Korea, what determines how they express anger is their perception and feeling about themselves.

In Asia, if you are of an affluent family and you feel like you have the power to do anything you want, expressing anger is much more comfortable because the society will acknowledge that you indeed have the privilege to do what you want. Therefore, anger is more likely to have positive outcomes for you.

However, in a place like the US, where anger is constantly judged as a negative emotion, and it is uncomfortable to express anger no matter what class you are from or the position you hold, you are more likely to have negative effects when you express anger.

Certain socio-cultural factors go a long way in altering how human biological processes work. So, if westerners stop judging anger or the expression of anger less harshly, it might improve the quality of health when anger is expressed.

In other words, when your culture makes you feel comfortable to express anger, you are less likely to feel bad about expressing this emotion.

The study further shows that anger is also impacted by how culture perceives individualism. In the western cultures of countries such as the United States, the United Kingdom, etc. the primary unit of the society is the individual.

The society exists to champion the interest of the individual and also his wellbeing. In the west, you are encouraged to be yourself, and you also have the freedom to express your feelings and opinions in order to influence others.

On the other hand, eastern cultures of countries such as Japan, Korea, China, etc. consider the group as the basic unit of the society. The eastern cultures expect people to express their feelings and opinions while considering the interest of the group. This is to promote harmony in society.

In a place like the US or UK, where much value is placed on individualism, the goal is for the individual to influence others. In Japan or Korea, where group harmony is valued much more than individualism, you are expected to adjust your feelings to conform to what others consider acceptable.

How you express anger also affects the people around you. It either encourages or discourages them from you.

Some cultures influence people in a way that they only express or experience emotions the society expects them to experience. People in the US express and react to anger more forcefully than Japanese because the culture promotes intense seeking emotions and engaging in activities that promote strong emotions such as anger.

Learning about anger is expressed and reacted to in different cultures can go a long way in helping you manage anger. Although you may think otherwise, anger doesn't have to adversely affect your physical or emotional health as long as you learn to focus attention where necessary.

Gender and Anger

If I happen to ask you a question like, "who is angrier between men and women?" what would your reply be? You are probably going to answer that men are often angrier than women, just like many other people would.

Although it may seem like a stereotype to say that men get angrier than women when there are certainly men who are usually as calm as the still sea, it is no stereotype that men actually express anger more than women.

The society has made anger into somewhat of a masculine emotion. So, it feels normal when you see a man express anger but terrifying when you see a woman do the same. For instance, if you are a fan of the Hip Hop industry, you may have an idea of what I'm talking about.

In pop culture, it is considered boss behavior when a male musician expresses anger while a typical female musician is usually considered bitter or angry when she expresses anger. This shows that anger has been normalized for men, while it is considered a taboo emotion for women.

For instance, the rap superstar Nicki Minaj is always in the media for reacting angrily to a triggering situation while someone like Drake may be commended for expressing the same emotion in the same kind of situation.

A stereotype has been established that anger is a more acceptable emotion in men than women. This may appear like an outdated view, but it unsurprisingly applies to a majority of the population.

In women, anger is often tagged "uncivil and unladylike" while it is labeled "powerful and dominant" in the opposite sex. In a family, parents are likely to teach the male child to be expressive and dominant while admonishing him never to cry like a baby.

So, the boy grows up with the belief that he is never to be emotionally weak. Thus, he learns to suppress feelings such as fear, envy, and jealousy while substituting them with anger.

Gender-based differentiation between men and women is a product of society and not of nature.

Here is one interesting thing you should know: studies have disproven the belief that men are usually angrier than women. In fact, some studies had actually shown that women are usually angrier when comparisons were made.

However, men are more comfortable with expressing anger because society accepts it from them. On the other hand, women feel angry, but they rarely express it because of how society views it. Women are more likely to express anger passive-aggressively while men are most aggressive with anger.

Fear, shame, envy, jealousy, and similar emotions are regarded as emasculating emotions. This makes men find it difficult to express them. Instead, they resort to anger because it gives a faux sense of control, which is what many people really struggle with.

The point is that it isn't okay to label anger as a masculine emotion or whatnot. Anger is neither a masculine nor a feminine emotion; it is just an emotion.

It doesn't matter whether you are a man or woman; you have the right to express anger healthily in any needed situation. Your emotions are nobody else's but yours. Therefore, you should be the one to decide whether you want to express the emotion or not.

Do not let anybody make you feel like you aren't supposed to get angry because you are a woman. Also, never let anybody make you think it is okay to express anger anyhow and anywhere whenever you are angry.

The idea is always to know that anger is meant to be expressed in healthy and safe ways. It is never okay to express anger unhealthily, but it is even worse if you choose to suppress and internalize anger.

No matter what society accepts, gender shouldn't be a tool for determining if anger is acceptable or not. As a natural emotion necessary for human survival, it is important to accept anger as an emotion for everyone and anyone, regardless of gender.

Anger in Children and Teenagers

As the normal humans that they are, children get angry just like everybody else. Everyone gets angry, so do kids. You shouldn't prevent a child from expressing anger when necessary. However, some kids are in a perpetual state of anger.

Children also have anger problems. A constantly angry child finds it difficult to enjoy life. You would find a child like this getting into fights when playing with their peers or doing something that is meant to be fun.

Angry children also resort to bullying others in order to disguise their own anger or possibly fear. So many factors can affect whether a child becomes angry or hostile. If not curbed from childhood, an angry child will likely grow into an angry adult.

Of course, it is okay for children to throw temper tantrums once in a while. But when tantrums become excessive and too intense, it means the child is likely dealing with an anger management problem.

As a parent, even you may find it difficult to understand the source of your child's anger. Even though many parents try to dismiss it as normal child behavior, parents always know when they have a problematic child on their hands.

Often, some parents also try to make excuses for anger behavioral problems in their children, claiming that it's all just children foolishness. There are parents who conclude that giving in to every demand made by a child is the way to manage temper tantrums, but this isn't so.

Other parents also delude themselves into believing the child's behavior is a normal one. They try to make it seem like it is appropriate for a child to vent and act aggressively because the child is simply 'expressing' his or her emotions. This happens even more with male children.

While it is true that children should be allowed to express themselves in order to teach them assertiveness in communicating their emotions, a parent should never disregard the possibility of their child having an anger problem.

But, there are also parents who genuinely can't tell when anger has spiraled out of control into a problem. They have no idea whether their children's behavior is normal or problematic. This doesn't matter, though.

The duty of a parent is to help their child learn the best and healthiest ways to express their emotions without resorting to tantrums or other aggressive tendencies.

As a parent, there are signs to watch out for if you want to know if your child has an anger problem. The first sign is to see if the child has a poor relationship with his friends and others. Once in a while, it is normal for one child to hit another or call them names.

However, if this becomes a constant occurrence, and it starts preventing your child from having solidified and healthy relationships with others, you may have an angry child on your hand. Make sure you tackle the problem immediately.

If you do not do this, such a child may grow up, finding it hard to build and maintain healthy, long-term relationships with other people.

If you notice or observe that your child's problematic behavior is starting to interfere with family life, it may be pointing to a possible anger issue in the child. No one in the family should have to walk on eggshells around a particular child in the family.

It means there is a problem somewhere if anyone in the family has to do this. Without a doubt, this could have a major impact on the relationships in the family; it is neither healthy nor appropriate for any member of the family.

You shouldn't have to give in to a child's demands in order to manage the problem; it will only make the problem harder as it is just a temporary solution. The child may become even worse in behavior.

Even worse, other members of the family may become resentful towards the child. If your child's behavior is making you miss out on important activities and one-on-ones, it could mean that there is a problem on your hand to tackle.

Some children start being aggressive right from a very little age. To these children, aggression is a tool for getting away with whatever they do or making their parents meet their demands. A child would never use aggression as a tool unless the child has an anger problem.

Normally, aggression should always be the last option for anybody. But, children with anger problems often act out more often than normal because they use this as a defense mechanism.

If your child finds it difficult to solve problems, resolve arguments, or seek help from others, the child may be using aggression as a defense mechanism, and you need to correct that as soon as you observe it.

Have you ever seen a 12-year-old child throw a temper tantrum, and it feels odd? Some tantrums are just not age-appropriate in certain children. It may be normal for a 3-year-old to throw a fit, but it sure isn't acceptable in a 10-year-old.

The older a child gets, the more the level and frequency of meltdowns and tantrums decrease. If you notice that your child's temper tantrums are getting worse instead of better, it is a pointer that the child has a problem in the regulation of his emotions. Thus, he needs to learn better.

Finally, having a low level of tolerance for frustrating situations is another sign to watch out for if you want to tell if a child has an anger problem. As a child matures, he or she should be able to develop an increased level of tolerance.

Watch your child and observe if he tends to get frustrated quickly when things aren't going his way. For instance, if he tears up his paper every time he makes a mistake on his school assignment. This means the child needs to learn to develop higher tolerance.

Anger is usually even worse when a child grows up to become a teenager. Teenage anger is a real issue. The teenage years come with raging hormones that make emotions harder to manage.

Teenagers get angry for a variety of reasons, and they express that anger in different ways. But, the one thing common with all teenage anger is that they never know how to manage or control that anger and the pain that comes with it.

A teenager who has no idea how to manage or cope with his anger problem may act impulsively on the feelings, without paying mind to the fact that anger could place him or other people at risk.

For teenagers, feelings of hurt, frustration, and unhappiness are usually the emotions beneath their anger. In the bid to avoid these emotions, a teenage usually resorts to anger because of the sense of control it gives.

What you should know if you have an angry teenager is that anger is not the problem. As you already learned in the book, anger is a normal and appropriate emotional response to certain feelings, so this doesn't make it a problem.

The problem is the inability of a teenager to cope with emotion is the problem here. Just like little children throw temper tantrums when they are unhappy, teenagers also try to deal with similar emotions by projecting it aggressively onto other people or situations.

To help a teenager struggling with anger, you must help them learn to recognize anger and find more constructive and healthier ways to deal with anger. Parents can do so much to help an angry teenager cope with anger.

As we progress in the book, I will elucidate more on how you can help children and teenagers manage their anger successfully.

Chapter Five

Anger Management

For many people, anger management is the ability to control feelings of anger whenever you experience it. But, what these people don't know is that anger management is much more than that.

Anger management, in totality, refers to the ability to identify, recognize, and manage impending symptoms of anger in order to take necessary steps to express the anger productively. Managing anger is not just about holding anger in or preventing yourself from expressing anger.

Anger is a healthy and productive emotion, an emotion that you should learn to express appropriately and healthily. This is exactly what you learn with anger management.

You may think otherwise, but anger management is actually quite easy to learn. It is easy to learn as long as you are willing to develop the necessary skills to help cope with those feelings of anger.

Anger management skills can be learned individually with the aid of books, resources, and other materials. Books such as this and other resources will help if you follow the information as you should. But, this is only if your anger management is in a moderate range.

If your anger is intense and too powerful, it is best to go for professional anger management class or professional therapy to effectively learn to manage your anger.

Anger is an old-age problem, and anger management dates back to thousands of years. So many notable figures have contributed to anger management right from time. Some of these people include Greek physician Aelius Galenus, Roman philosopher Lucius Annaeus Seneca, and Francis of Assissi.

All of these people are prominent figures who contributed to the development of anger management. In the modern age, some other trained psychologists such as Raymond Novaco, Howard Kassinove, and Peter Stearns also made major contributions to the development of anger management therapy and classes for people who need it.

The objective of anger management is to help people recognize the physiological and emotional signs that accompany the buildup of anger so that you can take productive measures to quell the anger.

With anger management, you get to understand that you aren't meant to hold anger in. Rather, you're meant to express it the best way possible. It is important to learn anger management if you find it difficult to cope with your anger.

Why is this? Anger management teaches you to recognize and resolve frustrations and other emotions that trigger your anger in order to help you stay in control while expressing your needs.

Many people don't believe or think that they need anger management even when they know fully that their anger is out of control. This may be because they grew up thinking of anger as an emotion that must be expressed in certain ways.

It may also be because anger is a learned behavior. There are people who, due to their childhood, believe that angry outbursts are very normal and vital for personal and professional relationships to thrive.

In fact, I once met a woman named Joanna, who believed anger was a necessary part of the world. According to Joanna, she grew up watching her parents argue, fight, and make up every day. Sometimes, the arguments led to physical assault, but they always made up anyway.

This made Joanna grow up, believing that it was normal for couples to fight in their relationships. Therefore, every relationship she got into, she always tried to instigate fights and drama, but of course, the relationships usually ended very badly.

Joanna was confused about why her relationships suffered since it never appeared like her parents suffered or anything like that. After all, they always ended up resolving the conflicts. For Joanna, anger had become a learned problem, and she always felt insecure if her partner wasn't fighting with her or getting angry for any reason at all.

I had to make Joanna understand the fact that it isn't normal to fight all the time in a relationship. Of course, couples would always have one or more issues that lead to conflict, but no one should feel uncomfortable just because their partner doesn't want to get into an argument or a fight.

No matter what the reason for your anger is or whether you think you need anger management or not, there are ways for you to tell if you need professional anger management. They are;

- Regular inability to contain your anger
- Persistent negative thought patterns and bizarre interpretation of negative experiences and events.
- Habitual feelings of annoyance, irritation, impatience, displeasure, and unfounded hostility.
- Occasional or regular aggressive tendencies with physical violence.
- Threats of abuse or violence against property or other people.
- Reckless and problematic behaviors are owing to anger.
- Avoidant behavior due to anxiety or unhappiness over your angry outbursts.

How does Anger Management work?

Anger management works in a defined and straightforward way, using a clear set of guidelines that you are to follow for recovery. As someone with an anger problem, you are treated in a controlled environment that provides room for the release of all your emotions.

Despite this freedom to express yourself as you wish, the goal of anger management is to help you learn how to give constructive reactions to these emotions, instead of destructive ones. When you go for anger management therapy, especially, your trained therapist encourages you to identify the trigger of your anger.

In other words, you are taught to become aware of your emotions and be conscious of how it rises to each state of arousal. When you learn this, it becomes quite easy to master the signs that accompany anger so you can control them and ultimately control anger.

In therapy, you are given insight into how your body reacts to past, present, and future events. This is achieved by teaching you to recognize the emotional reaction connected with a particular event or circumstance.

Your therapist would also help you recognize responses to anger, which may be serving as a protective or defensive mechanism against other problems. These problems could include anxiety, depression, and other mental health disorders like obsessive-compulsive disorder.

Anger management can really go a long way in solving the majority of your problems. For instance, if your social network has been suffering due to your anger problem, you can build it back up after you learn anger management.

This isn't all. Since anger doesn't affect only you, anger management is a way of helping the people closest to you and those included in your social network too. An inability to control anger can result in major psychological and physical consequences for you and the people around you.

Anger management teaches you to control anger so you can avoid these disastrous consequences. By going for anger management, you are also inadvertently managing stress. This lowers the possibility of you having any health problems such as heart disease, increased blood pressure, and the likes.

By learning anger management or going for anger management therapy, you can learn more positive, optimistic, and productive ways of interpreting any situation, whether positive or negative.

If the level of your anger is too intense for you to try to manage on your own using appropriate resources and you go for anger management therapy, there are a number of things you can expect in the classes.

Firstly, anger management may either take place individually or in groups. Anger management classes address certain anger issues, which could range from relationships to work-related anger. The therapy is usually on a continual basis.

The classes always come with home assignments and exercises for you to engage in. The homework and exercises complement the strategies and techniques that are being learned, class. They also give you the opportunity to practice what is being learned in therapy on your own.

For anger management to be successful, here are two key things you should fully immerse yourself in.

- Classes: At first, it may seem weird and maybe intimidating even to attend an anger management class, but remember that it is something you must do. In your classes, you will be learning important life skills to help you take control of your life.

Anger management classes are for you as long as your goal is to gain better control of your anger.

- Curriculum: There is various curriculum used in anger management classes. But, most of the curriculum is usually mapped out based on Cognitive Behavioral Therapy (CBT) strategies.

CBT is one of the leading psychotherapy for treating a range of problems, including anger management problems. It involves teaching the participants how to be aware of the signs that point to an impending angry outburst.

Cognitive-behavioral therapy employs the use of a number of relaxation strategies and techniques, which aim to change negative thinking patterns in order to change behavior.

The concept of CBT is that our feelings and behaviors are influenced by our thoughts. So, when you learn to make your thinking pattern positive, you also learn to change the feelings and behaviors that are being influenced. You will learn more about Cognitive behavioral therapy in a later chapter.

Steps in Anger Management

The first step in anger management is to recognize the triggers and signs (physical and emotional) that come before an angry outburst. This is the foundation of learning anger control.

First, you will have to make a list of the stressors that trigger or aggravate your anger. This could be frustration with your kids or a partner, financial troubles, or a bossy employer at work. Also, recognize the physical signs of when anger is rising.

This may be a racing heart, poor sleep, or clenched jaws and tightening your fist. Some emotional signs also include a need to scream out at someone or the feeling that you are holding something you really want to say in.

Next, you learn to manage the factors that make you prone to anger. For instance, you may start sleeping more in order to avoid feeling cranky and irritable.

Also, you will be taught to identify and recognize the situations that are likely to tick your time off so that you can prepare beforehand and react in nonviolent/nonaggressive ways. More importantly, you will be able to tell when you aren't thinking rationally in order to correct your thinking.

After this, you will also learn important skills that can come in handy when a situation is threatening to make you angry.

Anger management can be very advantageous. Once you are done with all of the stages involved in anger management therapy, you will be able to;

- Calm yourself down when necessary using relaxation techniques.

- Express your feelings and needs assertively even in situations that make you potentially angry.

- Concentrate on solving the problem in triggering situations instead of spending that energy on being angry.

- Use the most effective communication style to make your feelings known and solve problems.

There are so many benefits of going for anger management.

First of all, you can learn to communicate your needs effectively with anger management. You are able to talk about the things that bother you instead of expressing them in anger. The ability to express yourself effectively helps avoid impulsive behaviors.

This means you can avoid doing things you would later regret, such as yelling at a loved one, spewing hurtful words, acting aggressively towards another person, and many other things. Of course, this makes it easier to build and maintain positive relationships.

Another benefit of anger management is that it improves your health. Like I said, anger can have devastating effects on your health, so when you learn to manage it, you are improving your health.

Anger management also helps to prevent possible psychological and social problems. These include depression, anxiety, work-related problems, and troubled relationships.

One benefit of anger management, which I personally find interesting and helpful, is that it teaches you to use frustration to take care of things. Naturally, anger makes logical thinking almost impossible, if not impossible.

To avoid this, you can instead use frustration and anger as a motivating force to engage in productive activities and get important things done.

Learning anger management also helps you avoid resorting to addictive escapes to fight anger. Some people usually turn to drugs, alcohol, and other substances to suppress feelings of anger. To prevent this, the anger management techniques you learn will teach you to keep calm and in charge of your emotions, without the extra baggage.

How to Create Your Anger Management Plan?

An anger management plan is so essential because it makes anger management therapy much easier. Learning to control your anger with an anger management plan in place helps because it helps you learn faster and better.

Typically, an anger management plan should include the goals you aim to achieve by going for anger management. Of course, the primary goal is to learn how to control anger better, but you can make your plan much more specific.

Creating an anger management plan is very easy as long as you put your mind to it. If you need help controlling your anger, here are the necessary steps to follow;

• **Identify your goals in specifics:** This is the first thing you must do. Make sure you don't lay out your goal in a broad range; make it very specific in terms of behaviors and reactions. For instance: instead of saying, "I want to stop getting angry," say something like, "I want to stop getting angry when I'm criticized.

Also, measure your progress using an identified and specific timeframe. If your first goal is to stop getting angry when you are criticized, how do you measure this? Consider if you would be able just to take the criticism and walk away when it comes.

More importantly, make sure you estimate how much it would take you to master the art of keeping calm whenever criticism comes your way.

A typical goal will look like: Within the range of six weeks, I want to stop getting angry when I'm criticized.

• **Stop the blame game:** A plan doesn't have to be written to be a plan; you can also put it in mind. Another thing to include in your plan is a decision to stop blaming others for your anger reactions and behaviors.

Blaming others for your behaviors doesn't do much good because it doesn't make you less angry. Self-blame is even worse because it heightens feelings of resentment and anger, which only complicates the situation.

Take responsibility for your emotions, reactions, and behaviors in full like you should whenever things don't go your way.

• **Practice Relaxation Techniques:** Lastly, including calming and relaxation exercises in your plan is also very important. Learn important techniques and exercises to calm you whenever you are angry and ensure you engage in regular practice to hone your skills further.

Deep breathing, progressive muscle relaxation, guided imagery, visualization, and others are some of the relaxation exercises to include in your plan. I'll tell you more about how to practice each of these exercises in order to control anger better.

Finally, make sure you talk to important and relevant people as you move forward in your plan. Talking to the right people can go a long way in the quest to learn anger management and control.

Building a strong, support system is essential because it gives you the avenue to blow off steam and let out your feelings whenever you have to, through open and honest communication. Whoever you choose to discuss your feelings with, make sure it is someone you trust and have a healthy relationship with.

You can always learn to express your feelings and needs without resorting to anger as a tool for expressing emotions.

Chapter Six

Anger Management Techniques: 10 Step Guide

This book is entitled "10 steps guide to master your emotions" for a reason, and that reason is what you are about to find out.

In this chapter, I aim to share the ten practical steps I always share with anybody who wants to learn to control their anger. This chapter is going to be very practical because it contains actual steps for you to take in controlling your anger.

All ten steps I will be given to you have, in fact, been proven over and over by science-based research to really work for anger management.

Learning to manage anger can be both difficult and easy, depending on how much work you put in. It can be difficult in the sense that you will find it quite challenging to start utilizing each of the steps we will be talking about.

Habits are hard to change, and if your habit is to always make a big deal out of the most trivial issues, it will be hard to stop doing this and replace it with a healthier and more beneficial way of behaving in certain situations.

On the other hand, it can also be easy in the sense that all of the 10-steps guides I will be sharing with you are things that are pretty straightforward and direct. You can easily incorporate them into your lifestyle in order to facilitate the positive change you so much desire.

So, let's find out the ten important strategies in learning anger management!

1. Identify your Triggers

It probably sounds cliché already, but this is the first crucial step to learning anger management. If you are in the habit of ticking off and exploding on people like a time bomb, it is time to examine yourself and take a mental and physical note of the things that make you tick.

Anger is immediate, so you always tend to move immediately from a trigger to the reaction. This makes it hard even to know the trigger responsible for the anger. Anything can be a trigger for your anger.

It could be criticism from your boss at work, the children's incessant chattering while you are trying to concentrate on something important, a difficult homework from school, or a request from your parents to do something while you are immersed in something totally different.

The key is to know whatever triggers your anger and then find a way to stop letting that thing trigger you. Your trigger may be a person, an object, or certain situations. Keep in mind that identifying triggers doesn't mean blaming other people for your anger. It isn't the same.

The goal is to understand why that thing is a trigger so you can work on how to make it stop making you lose your cool.

One of the ways to know your triggers is to calm down and observe how your body responds whenever you are in a situation that could potentially trigger feelings of anger in you. Sure, you may not be able to recognize anger, but you can recognize the signs that come along with anger.

Even in anger management classes, you will learn that self-awareness is a vital tool for survival. And, nothing spells self-awareness more than an ability to recognize what makes you feel a certain way and what doesn't.

To deal with the issue of triggers, start by structuring your day in a way that manages stress without problems. Also, I always engage in quick anger management techniques before you encounter situations that you know to be distressing for you. This increases your fuse length and ensures one encounter of that trigger doesn't make you go off.

2. Know the Anger

Know your anger. How exactly do you know your anger? Well, you should be able to tell whether the anger you feel rising in you is a friend or an enemy when you feel the anger rising.

Sometimes, it helps to make sure you know what type of anger you are feeling before you take steps in calming yourself down and avoiding a reaction. Some anger is just very necessary and crucial to express, albeit healthily.

If you witness a fellow human's right being abused and you feel yourself getting angry, this means the situation and the circumstance aren't healthy, so this anger is justified. The anger is justified because the situation is an unjust one, and injustice is meant to make you angry.

Rather than calming yourself or using whatever technique to change your emotional state in that situation, what you need to do is channel that emotional state in a way that helps and address the situation you are faced with.

On the other hand, if you get in an argument with someone and the person says something to hurt your ego, thereby making you angry, you may need to do a quick check. If the anger is pushing you to lash out at the person or is making you uncomfortable, then you know that anger is an enemy.

In this case, it means you should do whatever is necessary to change your emotional state so you can address the issue with a calmer approach.

Knowing your anger means being able to understand the context of the situation you are in, where your anger is coming from, and if the anger is pushing you to react in a negative way or not. This will be quite easy once you learn the place the anger is really originating from.

3. Step Back from the Anger

If you examine the anger you are experiencing, and you understand that it is one that is pushing for a negative reaction, it means the next step is to take a step back from the situation and the anger.

This is indisputably one of the best ways to respond to anger triggers. Doing this gives you the time you need to recognize how the anger is building up so you can think clearly and logically before you react.

If you don't do this, it will be pretty easy for the anger or frustration to build up faster than you can control, and before you know it, the rage may become physical and destructive.

Taking a step back from anger halts the buildup of your anger in order to diminish the intensity. Stepping away from anger starts with stepping away from the situation fueling the anger. It always helps to take a break.

If you get into a heated argument, leave the conversation. If the meeting is getting hotter than you can handle and you feel like you are about to explode, make an excuse, and leave the meeting for a while.

A time-out is sometimes what your brain needs to register the situation and think clearly and rationally about what is happening.

Unfortunately, most people don't know how to step back from a situation whenever they are getting angry. Rather than step back, they feel like it's easier and more dominant to press the situation and lunge an attack,

The anger is usually so intense that it leaves them blind to certain constructive behaviors they can choose a response instead. The ability to step back from anger and a triggering situation start from self-control.

So, you would need to work on improving your self-control so as to be able to move away or step back from situations making you angry.

4. Choose your Reaction

What most people usually fail to realize is that there is always a choice to make when reacting to anger. I'll always say it to whoever cares to listen that the choices you make are what defines the kind of anger you express.

Anger in itself is just anger; it becomes destructive or constructive depending on the kind of reaction you respond to it with. Your reaction to anger is always a choice you make yourself, and the aim is to start making better choices when you are angry.

This particular step is quite easy to do, but it will never work if you don't incorporate the first three steps. You will learn to choose your reaction only after you know your trigger, know your anger, and take a step back from that anger so you can analyze the situation logically.

Stepping back from anger gives you the avenue to choose your reaction more carefully. Once you step back, think about it, and see the possible consequences of reacting in a certain way, you can react in a more appropriate way.

To choose the right reaction, you must learn to get rid of that urge to blame somebody else for your anger. Blaming someone else or a situation is just a way of making yourself the victim in your situation.

One thing you should know is that there is no single good choice for reacting to anger. The choice you make should be subjective to a number of factors such as the cause of the anger, the emotion you think is beneath the anger, your interpretation of the situation after you have taken a step back and logically analyzed the situation and a number of other factors.

Examine the situation carefully and determine the right reaction for you to make. No one can ever choose your reaction for you because no one has the ability to understand your anger as you can.

5. Exercise

Of course, the conversation would never be complete when talking about anything related to mental or emotional health without the mention of exercise. Why? Because exercise is an overall treatment for just about anything. You won't know this until you try it for everything, though.

Anger gives your body a rush of energy that needs to be used. This energy rush is usually what pushes you to react in certain ways, which you end up regretting. When you choose your reaction, one of the best ways to put the energy to use, so it doesn't consume you, is to engage in activities that require you to be mobile.

Be it a brisk walk down the street, complete cleanup of your home, or a quick visit to the gym, there is more than one way through which you can put the energy to good use and get rid of the extra tension in your body.

Regular exercises help you decompress i.e., get rid of pressure and stress. Remember that anger is sometimes a product of stress. So, when you exercise to get rid of the stress and pressure, you are also putting anger at bay.

Certain activities and aerobic exercises decrease your level of stress, which in turn improves your tolerance level so you can cope with anger and frustration better.

But, make sure you don't take exercise literally as running, jogging, or engaging in other aerobic exercises. In this context, exercising means doing anything that requires you to move your body, sweat a little, and burn off some unnecessary calorie or tension in the body.

The benefits of exercising are numerous, as much scientific research has pointed to. From increasing your mood to improving your overall wellbeing, there are so many things you stand to gain from engaging in tasking activities. So, why not take that bicycle and move down the street the next time someone at home makes you mad?

6. Change your Perception

Your perception of yourself and the world at large plays a major part in shaping how you interpret and react to emotions. So, what makes up your perception?

Your perception refers to your thoughts and the interpretation you give to these thoughts. Negative thoughts fuel negative feelings and negative reactions. Thus, when you think angry, you feel angry and act angry.

In an angry circumstance, if you keep thinking something like "I can't take this," or "I can't stand what she is saying," while the other person is talking, you are bound to get angrier and possibly react in a way you may end up regretting.

Some thoughts heighten frustration, and this, in turn, heightens anger. When you think about things that fuel anger, then you are definitely going to feel angrier.

In fact, the whole idea behind cognitive-behavioral therapy being employed as a strategy for anger management is the belief that thoughts influence feelings and behavior. So, if you encourage a negative thinking pattern in your mind, you are going to find yourself having more negative emotions and reacting mostly in negative ways to emotions.

If your perception of your workplace is that your colleagues are out to get you and they are intentionally doing things to make you angry, you will find yourself getting angry more times than you do on a normal.

This is because your mind is tricking your brain into believing that your thoughts are true, and there is indeed a perceived threat of danger. So, your brain activates the "fight or flight" response, which puts you in an angry state.

The only thing you can do is to change your perception and reframe your thoughts whenever you find yourself thinking about things that could fuel your anger. For example, if someone is criticizing you and you have a thought like "This person has no right to be saying this to me. I'm better than him," try changing your thoughts to something like, "This is just this person's opinion of me. I'm better than that, and he will realize that as time goes on."

Another angle to changing your perception is avoiding that rumination thinking pattern. Thinking over and over about an upsetting situation even after the situation is over will only make you aggravate your feelings of anger.

For instance, if you get into a fight with your colleague at work, thinking about the event as you return home from work might get you angry to a point where you take out the anger on your loved ones at home.

What you can do to avoid ruminating about a bad situation is to switch the channel in your head. The best way to change the channel in your mind is to get something energetic doing while you are angry, something to occupy your mind and chase away the thoughts.

7. Fish out the Underlying Feeling

As you already learned, anger is a secondary emotion. There is always one hidden or unidentified emotion behind anger. So, to manage anger effectively, start learning to fish out the undercover feeling behind your anger.

Hurt, pain, envy, jealousy, disappointment, unhappiness, and displeasure are some of the feelings that could be masquerading in the form of anger in order to avoid vulnerability. Anger is sometimes used as a mask to cover these feelings up.

Once you learn to identify the underlying feelings, it becomes easier to control your anger. You may be wondering how. When you deal directly with the primary feeling behind anger instead of anger itself, it means that you are addressing the problem from the root.

And, you know what they say about addressing a problem from the very root? It makes finding a solution much quicker. So, always ensure you know the primary emotion you are dealing with, so you can address that emotion directly and manage anger much faster.

Start by recognizing, acknowledging, and labeling these primary emotions before you take action on how to cope with them.

8. Seek a Solution

Anger management will never be effective for you if you don't learn to start seeking the solution to any situation you find yourself in. Instead of ruminating and concentrating on what made you mad, use that time and energy to find practicable solutions to the cause of your anger.

Seeking solutions also means working to resolve the argument or conflict on the ground. Let's say that stress is the major cause of angry outbursts in your life, and you want to manage that anger being fueled by stress.

Now, you identify and acknowledge the fact that your untidy room is the major stressor fueling your anger. The solution here is to clean up every bit of your room to a point where it no longer makes you feel tired or stressed.

Once you do this, the room would stop being a stressor, and your anger would definitely reduce.

Another side to seeking a solution is to talk about your feelings with a close and trusted friend. A solid support system can go a long way in helping a person who is learning to manage anger.

Make sure the person you share your thoughts and feelings with is someone that could calm you down whenever the rage is flying. Take note that talking in this context doesn't mean venting or complaining to this person.

It simply means talking about your needs, feelings, and thoughts in the healthiest and calmest way possible while this person listens. Also, keep it in mind that the person doesn't have to have a solution or advice for you.

Simply talking to whoever it is will clear your mind and give you a handle over your emotions so you can decide what next with a clear head and a sharp mind.

More importantly, make sure you are using it as an active avenue to find a solution when talking with a trusted friend. Think and seek for solutions even as you let your feelings and needs know.

9. Engage in a Rewarding Activities

In this context, rewarding activities refer to the things that make your mind feel at ease whilst also making your body feel good. Some people sometimes refer to drugs, alcohol, and substance abuse to fight anger. Of course, these activities sound rewarding, too, but are they really rewarding?

When I say rewarding, I mean doing things that your body is bound to appreciate you for. Get more sleep, eat better food, exercise more, and practice some relaxation exercises while you are at it.

There are several relaxation techniques out there for you to try. The only thing is to find one that is right and best for you. Certain breathing exercises and visualization techniques can really go a long way in helping you reduce tension while benefiting your body and mind.

The best part about these exercises is that most of them can be performed quite easily and discreetly. So, if you ever get into a heated argument at a meeting, all you need to do is step out for a while and quickly engage in a 2 min guided imagery exercise to bring back your mind to calm.

The kind of food you eat also has a large impact on your mood, feelings, and general wellbeing. Eat only foods that have the necessary nourishment for your body, mind, and brain.

Finally, get adequate sleep like science says you should. The eight hours of sleep for everybody to get in a day is 8. Make sure you aren't skipping an hour of sleep because your body actually requires it.

Good food, better sleep, and some exercise may be all you need to get those feelings in check and under your radar.

10. Forgive

Learn to forgive yourself and forgive others while you are at it. Anger is never generalized; it usually has a specific target to whom it is directed. If your anger is aimed at a particular person, object, or situation, it is time to let go of that anger and forgive whoever this person is.

Forgiveness releases anger so that it doesn't hurt you more or ruin your life. Bitterness and grudges are two of the many faces of anger.

Usually, they are linked to some hurt or pain from the past, which you may have refused to let go of. Bitterness fuels anger more than other emotions do. I have seen people who didn't think they were angry since they never experienced rage.

Unknown to them, the hurt, frustration, and everything else are channeling itself directly into bitterness instead of anger. Then, this bitterness morphs into internalized anger. If you hold grudges, you aren't hurting anybody else but yourself.

Don't keep grudges or allow bitterness to fester in your mind. Forgive everyone who has hurt you so your mind can live in peace. Do not internalize anger because it doesn't affect the person you are angry at or make the anger go away.

If you get into a misunderstanding with someone and they say something hurtful, let them know immediately. Talk about the issue; address it. If you don't address it immediately, it will grow and become something much worse.

Do not keep it in or let resentment grow. Communicating and talking about your needs and feelings is important. But, remember it is even more important to let go of the pain from the past and avoid being uncertain of the future.

Anger may serve a particular purpose for you. Some people have angry outbursts just to get others to give in to their demands. They use anger as a tool for manipulation. Others thinking aggressive anger is a way to let someone know they are serious about something.

Although aggression may tend to your needs in the present, it usually comes with major long-term consequences that end up being bigger than you. Therefore, it is very important for you to follow the 10-step guide in managing your anger effectively.

Note: Do you know what a calm-down kit is? This is something I like to recommend to people with anger problems.

If you are someone who gets angry easily because of stress and you tend to take out the anger on the people closest to you, creating a calm down kit can go a long way in helping your anger management strategies work more effectively.

To create a calm-down kit, you need to think of objects you can use to engage your senses. You can easily change your emotional state when you see, look, hear, smell, and touch things that are calming.

For example, you can make a kit with scented hand lotion, a photo of the still sea or a serene landscape, your favorite flavor candy, and a book on meditation. You might also include calming music or audio on breathing exercises.

Just make your calm-down kit portable so you can make use of it whenever you find yourself getting angry in any circumstance or situation.

Stress and Anxiety Reduction Techniques

It is no longer news to you that stress and anxiety are some of the major causes of anger, right? In fact, there is probably nothing that fuels anger more than stress and anxiety. Both emotions activate the "fight or flight" response, which alerts you to danger and keeps you in a state of anger.

So, learning to relieve stress and anxiety can be really helpful to your anger management journey. This is why I will briefly give tips on how you can achieve stress and anxiety relief in order to manage anger.

Meditation

Nothing is more soothing to the body than a quick meditation session when you feel overwhelmed by stress and anxiety. A few minutes of practicing meditation every day can help relieve stress and anxiety.

Research has shown that practicing meditation daily could alter the neural pathways in the brain, making your body more tolerance to stress.

Meditation is quite easy to do. Simply sit up straight on the chair or a mat with both of your feet touching the ground. Close your eyes. Place your concentration on chanting out a positive affirmation while your eyes are closed.

Focus on your breathing, too, by placing your hand on your belly in order to sync your breathing. Avoid concentrating on the thoughts in your head. Just focus on the positive affirmations you are reciting and your breathing.

Body scan

This is a blend of deep breathing and progressive muscle relaxation. Start by taking long, deep breaths slowly. Concentrate on breathing so that your mind becomes detached from distracting thoughts and feelings.

After a few minutes of breathing deeply, focus on the part of the body mentally, and release any tension you feel there with your mind.

A body scan can be really helpful in boosting your awareness of the connection between your mind and body.

This technique is really useful if a particular part of your body is causing you pain or ache. It helps address the pain in that particular part.

Tune in to your body

Make it a habit to always tune in to your body after a long day of stress. Tuning in to your body means scanning your body each day to see how it's been affected by stress.

Sit up straight with your feet on the floor, or lie on your back. Start by concentrating on your feet and walk up to your scalp while noticing every sensation in your body.

Be aware of wherever you feel tension without attempting to correct anything. For a minute or to imagine your deep breaths flowing to each body part, you are focused on.

Repeat until you are done with every part of your body.

Yoga, Tai Chi, and Qigong

You do not know what you are missing out on if you have never had a session of either of these three ancient arts. Yoga, Tai Chi, and Qigong combine a series of movements with rhythmic breathing.

This avails you the opportunity to focus mentally and distract your mind from certain thoughts. All three also help enhance balance, flexibility, and mobility.

However, they can be really challenging for someone who hasn't been physically active in a while. Make sure you consult with your doctor before you start either.

Chapter Seven

Anger Management Exercises

A book on anger management will be incomplete without a chapter exclusive to training you on how to engage in different anger management exercises to help you cope with anger, stress, anxiety, and depression better.

I will be talking only about the five most effective exercises for calming and relaxing your mind so you can manage anger much better than you usually do. These are;

- Breathing Exercises

- Progressive Muscle Relaxation

- Guided Imagery

- Creative Visualization

- Mindfulness Meditation

The one thing common with all these exercises is that they aim at calming the mind, relaxing the body, and getting rid of overwhelming, negative thoughts. Let's talk about each technique one by one and how you can practice them.

Breathing Exercises

In professional anger management therapy, you will be trained in breathing exercise practice. Breathing exercises are very effective for managing stress, anxiety, and anger. There are different breathing exercises you can engage in, but we will be looking at three that could really help you.

• **Deep Breathing:** This is a particular breathing exercise that is effective for releasing tension and providing relief to your body and calm to your mind. It is also referred to as belly breathing or diaphragmatic breathing.

Deep breathing lowers blood pressure and relaxes tense muscles. So, how do you perform deep breathing, it's quite simple.

Firstly, find a quiet and comfortable place for this exercise. Make sure it is a place where you can't be distracted. Sit straight up on the floor while keeping your feet on the ground. Ensure you close your eyes.

Next, put one hand on your belly with the other on your chest so you can keep track of your breathing. First, take a normal breath. Then, take a long, slow deep breath. Use your nose to breathe in slowly and observe as your stomach swells up under your hand.

For a second, hold your breath and pause. Then, breathe out slowly through your mind. Again, pay notice to your stomach as it deflated under your hand again.

Do this over and over until you have a soothing rhythm.

Continue to do this for as much as 10 minutes until you feel fully relaxed, and the tension/stress is out of your body.

More importantly, make sure you pay attention to the multiple sensations your body brings as you breathe in and out.

- **Breath Focus:** This is a breathing exercise that combines the use of imagery with breathing. You can also focus on a certain word or phrase instead. Ensure it is a word/phrase that brings a smile to make your face and makes you feel relaxed.

Firstly, find a quiet place where you can sit or lie down comfortably without distractions.

Start by breathing gently and bringing your awareness to your breaths. Do not attempt to change your breathing pace.

Switch between regular and deep breaths occasionally. Observe the difference between regular breathing and deep breathing. Notice how your belly expands with the deep breathes.

Put a hand on your belly button so you can observe the sensations in your stomach as you breathe. Engage in deep breathing for a few moments and let out a loud sigh every time you exhale.

Every time you breathe, focus on your chosen word, phrase, or picture, which depicts calm and relaxation.

The imagery you imagine could be of the air you are inhaling and exhaling washing away the tension in your body. You can also choose a phrase like "Absorbing peace and calm."

• **Pursed Lip Breathing:** A very simple breathing technique aimed at slowing down the pace of breathing. All you need to do is put deliberate effort into every breath you take until your mind is no longer racing, and you are no longer breathing faster than normal.

The best thing about pursed-lip breathing is that you can practice it at any time. To become very good at pursed-lip breathing, you must practice at least four times a day until you master the breathing pattern.

To begin, relax your shoulders and neck first. Make sure your mouth is closed, then slowly inhale through your nose two times.

Make sure your lips are pursed as you breathe through the nose. Now, exhale the air through your pursed lips at each count of 4.

Do this for as long as you can until you feel relieved of stress, and your breathing is back to normal.

Progressive Muscle Relaxation

Again, this technique helps manage anger by relieving stress and tension in the body. It also works if you have a nagging pain or ache in whenever you feel stressed. Muscle tension is a response the body gives whenever you are stressed and tense. This could result in feelings of anger. So, progressive muscle relaxation helps relieve muscle tension so as to prevent anger.

This technique works by tensing a group of muscles as you inhale and then relaxes them as you exhale. It works on muscle groups following a certain order. The more you practice progressive muscle relaxation, the better you get.

You may start with the use of an audio recording so as to aid your memorization of the muscle groups. Once you know the muscle groups, you can do everything on your own. The best thing about this method is it also helps improve sleep. So, it is really effective all round.

To practice progressive muscle relaxation, follow these steps;

- Find a quiet, calm place where you can't be disturbed by anybody or anything. Make sure it is somewhere you can lie comfortably on your back and stretch out without hindrances. For instance, you may practice on a carpeted floor.

- Breathe in slowly, and tense your first muscle group hard for about 10 seconds. Try not to tense the muscle group to the point of pain, though.

- Now, breathe out suddenly, and release the tension on the muscle group. Do it suddenly, and not gradually to make the effect immediate.

- Relax for 20 seconds before you progress to your next muscle group. Observe the difference between the feel of your muscles when they are tensed and when they are relaxed.

- When you are done with all muscle groups, count back from 5 to 1 to bring your awareness back to the present.

Muscle Group

What to do

Forehead

Squeeze the muscles for 15 seconds, then release and relax for 30 seconds or more.

Neck and shoulders

Shrug your shoulders by raising them up towards your ears and stay like this for 15 seconds. Then, release and relax for 30 seconds.

Jaw

Tense them by breaking into a very wide smile. Make it as wide as you can. Do this for 15 seconds before you release and calm down for another 30 seconds.

Arms and hand

Slowly draw your hands together and clench them into fists. Pull the fists to your chest while squeezing as tight as possible. Release after 15 seconds and relax for 30 seconds before you move on.

Buttocks

Squeeze your buttocks tightly together in a tensed position. Do this for 20 seconds and then release the tension. Relax for some seconds before you go on to the next muscle.

Legs

Curl your toes while pointing them towards your face. Then, point them away from your face. Slowly, increase the tension for about 15 seconds while squeezing the muscles as hard as you can. Release the tension after 15 seconds and feel it melt away.

Feet

Increase the tension in your feet and toes by curling them upwards and downwards. Make the muscles really tight, then release the hold on the muscle group. Slowing breathe in a balanced way as you release the tension.

Savor the feelings of relaxation that sweeps through your body as you finish with all the muscle groups. Note that it is always helpful to precede progressive muscle relaxation with a quick deep breathing exercise that sets your body in order.

Guided Imagery

Guided imagery is an exercise that combines focusing on all your five senses to activate positive sensations all through your body and mind. Many people confuse guided imagery for visualization, but they are somehow different.

Both techniques involve the use of imagination with your five senses, but the difference is that guided imagery has laid down mental images to follow. The images are premeditated and guided. On the other hand, visualization is creative. You have the choice to create whatever imagery you want in your mind as long as it is something that makes you feel calm and relaxed.

This is not to say that visualization cannot be guided too, though; it can be guided or unguided. But guided imagery is always guided. It is directed with the use of audio, video, or written script.

With guided imagery, you use your sight, sound, smell, taste, and touch to create images in your mind, which your body feels are as real as actual events. The action doesn't take place in the body, though; it does in mind, using mental visualization. But, the sensation goes into your body.

Firstly, you should know that guided imagery usually involves either of these three images: a tropical beach, soothing waves of the ocean, or the warm sun. But, if you think there is an imagined scene much better for you, then make use of that imagined scene in your practice.

The scene is not as important as immersing yourself fully in the imagination with the use of your sight, smell, and sound to take yourself to the imagined destination.

Follow these steps to practice guided imagery using an imagined scene of the tropical beach;

- Find a comfortable place for practice. Make sure this place is quiet, calm, and without disturbances that could jolt you out of your imagination. Lie on the floor or sit in a reclining chair.

- Get rid of any tight apparel and remove any lens or contacts.

- Place both of your hands on your lap or on the arm of the chair you are seated in.

- Before you begin visualizing, engage in deep belly breathing for some minutes. This is to calm your mind so you can find it easier to visualize whatever you want to.

- Once you are feeling relaxed, close your eyes. Now, imagine yourself on a beach with nobody else, preferably a secluded one. Visualize soft white sand all around you.

- Picture the crystal-clear waters of the beach and a cloudless sky with the breeze blowing gently behind you.

- Keep your eyes closed as you imagine this beautiful scene in your mind.

- Time to use your sense of smell and hearing. Inhale slowly and savor the scent of the waters and the tropical flowers. Hear the sounds of sea waves rolling gently onto the shire as some birds chirping in the palm trees.

- Feel the warmth of the sand beneath your feet and the sunshine on your skin. Imagine the taste of a soothing tropical drink in your mind. Do not just picture this. Ensure you are also tasting, smelling, touching, and tasting the scene. Feel the flowers on your fingers.

- Observe the feelings of calm and relaxation you now feel and let it spread all over your body. Enjoy the sensation it brings throughout your entire body, from head to toe. Stay in your imagined scene for as long as you want.

- Once you feel calm and relaxed enough, slowly bring yourself back to the present by counting back from 10 to 1. Then, open your eyes and take in your surroundings. Surely, you will feel that a state of calm has replaced whatever stress, anxiety, or anger you were feeling before.

- Work on letting this state of calm last throughout the rest of your day.

If you find it difficult practicing guided imagery by using a written script, you can consider the use of an audio recording that gives instructions on how to practice guided imagery. This will help you fully relax while concentrating on the techniques.

Creative Visualization

When you think of visualization, what comes to mind? Do you just think of conjuring certain images and boom; you are okay like it's magic? Or is it something else?

Well, visualization is more than just mentally conjuring images. You must be willing to focus and engage your senses. It is not just about seeing pictures in your mind. There is more than one way to visualize, but I will be talking about two exercises you can try.

Meditation and visualization are quite different, although some people tend to think they are the same. Visualization is a form of meditation, but it is more than just meditation. When practicing visualization, always remember that it is more than just seeing pictures in your head.

Visualization is most effective when you make it a multi-sensory activity. You also have to be creative enough to imagine something that really has a calming and relaxing on you. So, here are two visualization exercises you can practice.

• **Candle visualization exercise:** This involves visualization with a candle.

Gently close your eyes. Visualize that when you open them, there is a lit candle in front of you. Put in important details such as the size of the candle and the kind of candle it is.

Is it heavy? How much of the candle is left burning? Is it a newly lit candle, or it is almost down to the base?

Is the candle far away from you, or is it close, within arm's length? As you visualize, make sure you put effort into addressing every minor detail.

By the time you are done visualizing the kind of candle it is, all the stress and tension in your body should have evaporated.

Another thing is to light a candle before you start visualization. Gaze into the candle and then close your eyes. You will feel the sensation of the burning candle even as your eyes are closed.

● **Apple visualization exercise:** The candle exercise is just the visual aspect of visualization. The more you practice it, the better you get at creating the details of your candle and even making a flame of your own.

Once you have mastered this, take it a step further and embody your other senses. Start by visualizing an apple.

Use your sense of touch to feel the peel of the apple and then picture yourself taking a bite out of the apple. Notice the taste in your mouth. Take it up a notch by feeling the apple travel down your body.

Mindfulness meditation

Mindfulness meditation is a kind of meditation that has been proven by several studies to be of immense benefit to the mind and the body. It is a kind of mental training that teaches you self-awareness by focusing your mind on your experiences, emotions, thoughts, and sensations in the present.

Mindfulness practice may combine breathing exercises with visualization, imagery, and muscle relaxation.

This particular meditation helps very much with anger management because it trains you to become aware of your emotions, including anger before they jump on you. It also teaches you to focus on the present without giving any thought to the past or the future and also to accept everything without judgment.

Some of the benefits of mindfulness, which has been proven by science, are;

● Mindfulness improves wellbeing. Practicing mindfulness on a daily has a lot of positive impact on your wellbeing. Being aware of the present and staying grounded in it makes it impossible to get caught up in regrets over your past or uncertainties about the future.

People who meditate regularly are likely to be more concerned with success and have healthy self-esteem.

They also find it easy to create deep, meaningful relationships with other people.

● It promotes physical and emotional health. In more than one way, mindfulness has been proven to improve physical health by relieving stress and anxiety, lowering blood pressure, reducing chronic pain, and improving sleep.

Mindfulness also improves mental and emotional health by helping you to treat mental health problems like depression, addiction, social disorders, anxiety disorders, anger, and obsessive-compulsive disorder when combined with professional therapy.

Mindfulness meditation can be practiced in a number of ways. But, no matter the technique you use in practicing mindfulness, the aim of the exercise is to achieve a state of awareness, alert and focused relaxation.

To engage in mindfulness meditation, here are the steps you can follow

- Get a quiet, comfortable, and noiseless place for practice. You can either use a chair or sit on the floor. Wherever you decide to sit, ensure you sit in an upright position with your back straight but not stiff.

- Clear your mind of all thoughts of the past or future while immersing yourself completely in the present. Stay grounded in the present.

- Draw your awareness to the rise and fall of your breath, observing the sensation that the air moving in and out produces in your body as you breathe. Focus on the rise and fall of your belly and the in and out of the air in your nostrils and the mouth. Pay mind to the change in rhythm as you inhale and exhale.

- Become aware of your thoughts as they come and go. Do not judge whatever it thought is, be it fear, worry, frustration, anxiety, or anything. Just observe as the thoughts float around in your mind. Note that you shouldn't try to suppress the thoughts or ignore them. Simply make a mental note of them while focusing on your breathing.

- If you notice yourself getting carried away in the thoughts, don't judge yourself. Simply return your mind to your breathing after taking note of the thoughts. Don't be harsh with yourself.

- Once you are nearing the end of your meditation session, stay seated for one or two minutes and gradually become aware of your immediate environment. Appreciate the surrounding for a while and then slowly get up.

- Go about your day with your mind at rest.

In practicing mindfulness meditation, you can also incorporate it into other activities like doing the dishes, driving, exercising, or even brushing your teeth. Mindfulness is best practiced right before you go to sleep or when you just wake up.

Chapter Eight

Anger Management with Emotional Intelligence

In recent years, emotional intelligence has become a quite popular trend as most people like to call it. However, emotional intelligence isn't a trend. It is real, and it is something that is going to be around for as long as humans exist.

Emotional intelligence is a part of you, not an external factor or anything. To use emotional intelligence for managing and coping with your anger, all you need to do is hone and develop the emotional intelligence skills that are already inherent in you.

The definition of emotional intelligence is actually very simple. It is just the ability to recognize, identify, and understand emotions. It also involves the ability to use your understanding of your emotions to guide your actions, which means you can use it to cope effectively with anger.

Emotional intelligence isn't just about understanding your own emotions, though. It also involves being able to recognize and understand the emotions of other people. This lets you know what to say and how to react to them in certain situations.

Once you sharpen your emotional intelligence skills, it becomes possible to understand the context of any situation you find yourself in. Sometimes, we react angrily in certain situations because we don't actually understand the situation.

For instance, if you witness someone being attacked, and you perceive that injustice is happening in that situation, you may want to react angrily. But, the thing is that the situation has its own background and context, which you do not know.

When you recognize this fact, you learn never to jump into some situations without fully understanding the context and story behind the situation, and this keeps you from getting angry without a justifiable reason. That exactly is what you get from becoming an emotionally intelligent person.

I like to say that emotional intelligence is the ability to get angry for the right reason, at the right person, in the right context, in the right degree, at the right time, and in the right way. This really sums up what emotional intelligence is really about.

Another thing about emotional intelligence is that it entails the ability to channel your emotions using the right avenue, which is a healthy and assertive one.

Let me give you an example. If you go out to spend time with your girlfriend and instead of having a good day, you both get into an argument. Frustrated, you leave the place and return home.

On getting home, you meet your younger sister with your iPad, which you have warned her never to operate in your absence again. Angrily, you yell at her and ask what she is doing with your device even after you told her not to go near it anymore.

In this case, the reason for your anger seems like the iPad your sister operated without your permission. But, deep within yourself, is that really the anger for yourself? Of course, it may seem like the obvious reason, but you know that the actual reason is the argument you had with your girlfriend.

The feeling of frustration you carried over from the disagreement with your girlfriend is what you are letting out by venting at your sister. Thus, you are channeling your anger at the wrong time, through the wrong means.

Assuming you were emotionally intelligent, you would have learned never to vent your anger at your sister because she really isn't the cause of your anger. If you thought about the situation in an emotionally intelligent way, you would also be able to understand that your sister didn't operate your iPad because she wanted to make you mad. All she wanted to do was play.

The better you get at using emotional intelligence to understand why people do certain things or say certain things, the better you get at managing your anger successfully.

Looking at that example again as an emotionally intelligent person. On getting home to see your sister with the iPad and you get annoyed naturally, the first thing you'd do is understand that the annoyance is coming from a place of frustration which was caused by the argument you had.

Immediately you recognize the simple fact that your anger is a result of that argument, you also understand that your sister has no fault because she is a kid, and kids will obviously be kids.

Lack of emotional intelligence can affect a lot of things. It messes with your ability to manage your emotions because you don't even know these emotions. You can't regulate your emotions if you don't even know what that emotion is.

Using emotional intelligence, you can always tell the primary emotion underneath your anger whenever you sense yourself getting angry.

Developing your emotional intelligence opens your mind so you can always have a balanced view of any situation. As an emotionally intelligent person, you learn to think things through before you act.

Emotionally intelligent people never do something without thinking of the consequences first. So, how exactly do emotionally intelligent people react in a heated situation that is fueling anger? They leave.

It looks really easy to do when you think of it in your mind, but this is one thing that is actually hard to do when you are in an uncomfortable situation. Just like it is hard to leave a relationship when you love your partner so much, it is also hard to be the bigger person and leave a situation when it is pushing you to anger.

To sharpen your emotional intelligence, though, practice leaving any situation that is triggering and volatile. The more you practice doing this, the better you get at leaving the next situation.

Always leave a situation that is making you angry to avoid saying or doing something that you could regret. You will thank me later for this tip.

After leaving, take some moments to do a quick deep breathing exercise in order to get your emotions back to normal.

These are three skills you need to develop in order to become emotionally intelligent;

- The ability to recognize your emotions (emotional awareness)

- The ability to channel these emotions into something productive

- The ability to recognize, influence, manage and regulate the emotions of others.

Once you work on developing all three skills, anger management becomes as easy as pie!

Chapter Nine

Cognitive Behavioral Therapy

I want to believe that you have heard of cognitive behavioral therapy a number of times. I say this because it is another recent concept in pop psychology culture. Nowadays, cognitive behavioral therapy has become the go-to therapy for a number of mental health conditions.

Cognitive-behavioral therapy is a form of talking psychotherapy that follows a meditated, structured, and orientated procedure to help patients deal with mental health disorders and problems.

It was formulated based on several research, theories, and techniques that have all been proven by science actually to work.

It is based on cognitive and behavioral theories that specify thoughts as the catharsis of emotions and negative behaviors. The goal of cognitive behavioral therapy is to help you learn how to replace your negative emotions and behaviors by changing your thoughts from positive to emotion.

CBT, as it is shortly referred to, is a highly effective treatment for anger disorders and problems because of the techniques and methods it combines. Usually, CBT for anger management includes a number of procedures like; mindfulness training, cognitive restructuring, emotion regulation training, distress tolerance training, and assertiveness skill development.

Cognitive-behavioral therapy works by changing the way a person thinks. It trains you to get rid of negative and self-defeating beliefs so you can learn to solve your problems on your own.

It also changes the way you think and reacts to certain situations, triggers, and instances. It helps you get rid of feelings of stress, anxiety, and depression. Thus, it makes you feel less fearful, which in turn decreases how often you feel angry.

Another thing CBT does is to change how you act, react, and behave in situations where your feelings have been aroused. With CBT, an individual can learn to start having angry outbursts less, eating less, or going out less. In short, it aids you in changing those behaviors you don't like in yourself.

Interestingly, CBT also works for physical problems, just like it works for the mental and emotional ones. The therapy can help you if you want to get rid of back pain, ache, or anything else, causing discomfort in the body. This explains why it is used in the treatment of Obsessive-compulsive disorder.

In CBT, the therapist focuses on the present situation instead of trying to understand the past. This is one reason why it is different from other traditional therapies. The therapist offers techniques that focus on your perception of life, the beliefs, and the behaviors you exhibit.

In doing this, he or she attempts to solve your behavioral anger problems by replacing existing beliefs with new ones. For example, if you have the mindset that fighting in a relationship is normal and necessary, CBT would change this belief and replace it with a new one that says that it is unhealthy to fight in your relationships all the time.

The studies that have been conducted on how to manage anger with cognitive-behavioral therapy have a number of submissions on how to use CBT to deal with anger. According to these studies, anger becomes stronger and more powerful whenever you let it take control of your thoughts and actions.

Therefore, you must stop anger from becoming more powerful by taking control of your thoughts and actions from it. But how do you do this? The one thing you must do is learn to keep your reactions in balance with anger triggers. Never blow your reactions out of proportion because this is unreasonable.

What to Expect in CBT Therapy?

Cognitive and behavioral therapy techniques combine a range of exercises and questions with helping you fully assimilate the triggers, which fuel the intensity of your anger. When you master these triggers, you then learn to react to them in constructive and healthy ways.

When you do this, your therapist teaches you a number of techniques to experiment with to discover the solution to your anger problem.

CBT therapy is usually brief, short, and focused, so you can achieve a lot in just a little time. This is one of the reasons why it is highly effective and preferred over other traditional psychotherapy.

A therapy session may last for as long as 50 minutes with a series of weekly or fortnightly sessions. In all, the therapy will be between the range of 4 and 20 weeks, depending on what you agree on with your therapist.

As you progress in therapy, you can develop your ability to manage anger with new and more productive exercises. By the end of a good anger CBT therapy, you would have learned how to communicate your needs without resorting to anger assertively.

Here is a snippet of how to use CBT techniques to manage anger;

First, you learn to deal with your feelings. In the physiology of anger, the responses and feelings always come before you can even think clearly about the situation you are in.

Anger is automatic, so start by dealing with the automaticity of that emotion. One way you can do this is always to catch it before it sneaks on you. Practice making yourself angry and then quickly stop yourself just before you react angrily.

Simply think about something that once made you very angry and then catch yourself before you really become angry. Immediately you do this, use a relaxation exercise to calm yourself down. Anger is so powerful that you might actually get angry just by thinking about an event that once made you angry.

Benefits of CBT

CBT starts by helping you identify the source of your anger and the thing that fuels anger intensity whenever you get in a tensed situation. With CBT, you also learn how to decrease the overwhelming physiological responses your body gives when you have an angry reaction.

You also learn to replace angry behaviors and actions with clear and assertive communication, which actually achieves much better results. Your therapy sessions would also teach you to channel your anger positively in order to benefit your relationships and wellbeing.

Most importantly, CBT will teach you to express anger in healthy, constructive, and beneficial ways.

Conclusion

Anger may be a natural and necessary emotion, but you should never let it consume you. This is exactly what I hope you have learned through the duration of this book.

Managing your anger is very necessary if you want to live a normal, healthy, and fulfilling life with your personal and professional relationships intact.

In the book, I have taught you why anger is a necessary emotion and how you can channel it productively to accomplish your goals. More importantly, you had learned how anger can become destructive when not channeled the right way.

I talked about why anger isn't a bad or good emotion and how your choice is what makes anger positive or negative.

The book talked about the different ways anger can be channeled as a motivating force to get things done. I also touched on how anger is a secondary emotion and the different methods you can use to deal with the underlying emotion beneath anger.

Overall, I have informed you of a 10 step strategy that is very effective for anger management and how you can incorporate it into your life in order to start expressing anger more constructively and healthily.

Like I promised, this book has shown you the best and most effective relaxation techniques for working on anger and managing your emotions in both short-term and long-term.

You also learned about anger management therapy, CBT, and emotional intelligence skills, all of which can be used in your quest to become the master of your emotions and start living the best life possible.

I am sure you have learned more than enough in this book to get you started on the journey to an anger-free life. As an extra, this book will also help you conquer stress and anxiety if you have been dealing with them.

One thing I want you to take away from this book is that anger is a normal and healthy emotion, which you should never ignore, suppress, or express destructively. Always find ways to express your anger in the healthiest and most expressive ways possible.

CPSIA information can be obtained
at www.ICGtesting.com
Printed in the USA
LVHW080025240520
656396LV00006B/512

9 781913 597023